From The Hidden
FINAL EDITION

ANNE T. GARCIA

From The Hidden— You Will Understand It PERFECTLY
Copyright © 2004, (Xulon Press) Anne T. Garcia
Copyright © 2005 (Waymaker Publishers) Anne T. Garcia;
Revised 2006 - Copyright © 2006 by Anne T. Garcia

From The Hidden **FINAL EDITION**, Revised Copyright ©
2014 - Anne T. Garcia

Author's contact information:
Anne T. Garcia
Theresa Garcia Ministry - www.theresagarciaministry.com

Dedication

To all the wonderful people who watch the television show,
"Understanding The End Of The Age",
I look forward to meeting you all in glory!

TABLE OF CONTENTS

INTRODUCTION

W hen the Lord spoke to me in 2003 to "write a book", I understood the subject was to be this: To identify the Four Horsemen of the Apocalypse. In those days the popular definition of the four horsemen was:

White horse: Antichrist

Red horse: War

Black horse: Famine

Green (pale) horse: Islam, or a nebulous term, "death and hell"

Based on the Biblical principle that "in the mouth of two or three witnesses is every word confirmed", I believed we had to find a second reference to the four horsemen

Matthew 24	Revelation 6
⁴and Jesus answered and said to them: "Take heed that no one deceives you. ⁵"for many will come in My name, saying, 'I am the Christ,' and will deceive many.	verses 1 & 2 First Seal: Antichrist (white horse)
⁶"And you will hear of wars and rumors of wars. See that you are not troubled; for all these things must come to pass but the end is not yet. ⁷"For nation will rise against nation, and kingdom against kingdom	verses 3 & 4 Second seal: War (red horse)
⁷ᵇAnd there will be famines,	verses 5 & 6 Third seal; Famine (black horse)
7b (continued) pestilences, and earthquakes in various places. ⁸"All these are the beginning of sorrows. ⁹"Then they will deliver you up to tribulation and kill you, and you will be hated by all nations for My name's sake.	verses 7 & 8 4th Seal: Death & Hell (green horse)

somewhere in the Word of God. Some scholars point to the Olivet Discourse and find another reference to the Four Horsemen there. I would agree (see chart on page 10).

However, the four horsemen are extremely significant. After all, they are commanded to ride by the four living creatures when Jesus breaks the seals in heaven. This begins the seven year Tribulation. Therefore, one would expect to find the four horsemen somewhere else as well.

It is my view that the Books of Daniel, Zechariah and Revelation are the three great pieces of the end time puzzle. Let's consider for a minute the Books of Daniel and Revelation. There are startling similarities between these two authors and their work.

COMPARE THE LIVES OF
DANIEL AND APOSTLE JOHN:

1. Both men were highly favored of God: Daniel was called "greatly beloved" three times (Daniel 9:23; 10:11; 10:19). John was called the "disciple that Jesus loved" (John 19:26; 20:12; 21:7; 21:20) in the Gospel of John.

2. Both men were advanced in age when the future "end of days" was revealed to them.

3. Both men were exiled when they saw these events: Daniel in Babylon; John on the Isle of Patmos.

4. Both men saw the coming of the Lord in glory to receive His Kingdom (Daniel 7:13,14; Revelation 11:15-18; 19:11-16).

5. Both men were given the length of time of the Great Tribulation as 3 ½ years (Daniel 9:27: Revelation 13:5)

6. Evil men tried to kill both of these prophets. Daniel was thrust into a lion's den and John into boiling oil.

7. Both men died in their old age of natural causes.

The point is that the Books of Daniel and Revelation are parallel books written for the same purpose: To discuss the end of man's dominion of planet earth and the beginning of God's eternal reign. Daniel identifies the four nations that abuse the Jews during the times of the Gentiles in chapter 2 as Iraq, Iran, Greece and Rome. His second mention of these four nations is in Daniel 7. If the Books of Daniel and Revelation are parallel books, then John should also reference the four ancient enemies of Israel. Does John also identify Iraq, Iran, Greece and Rome?

We see when we read the Book of Revelation that there is only one set of four "bad guys" in this book. It is the Four Horsemen of the Apocalypse. In other words, if John names Iraq, Iran, Greece and Rome, they must be the Four Horsemen of the Apocalypse. Are they? That is my view.

The other "piece of the end time puzzle" is the Book of Zechariah. It is interesting to note that Zechariah 1 lists four horses and chapter 6 discusses the "four chariots". (In Zechariah's time men went to war in chariots. By the time John came on the scene, men had developed better saddle technology, including the stirrup. Therefore, men also went to war on horseback.) The point is that both Zechariah and Daniel reference the four enemies of Israel and the Jews. Therefore I expect John to mention them as well.

The question is: Are the four chariots of Zechariah 6 and the Four Horsemen of the Apocalypse two separate witnesses to the same groups of people? My answer to that question is "yes".

It is interesting to note that the first mention of the four chariots occurs in Zechariah 6:1-3:

> *[1] Then I turned and raised my eyes and looked, and behold, four chariots were coming from between two mountains, and the mountains were mountains of bronze. [2] With the first chariot were red horses, with the second chariot black horses, [3] with the third chariot white horses, and with the fourth chariot dappled horses—strong steeds.*

What are the "mountains of bronze?" The majority of the outstanding commentators agree these two "bronze" mountains are the Temple Mount and the Mount of Olives in Jerusalem. The question then becomes: What were representatives of Iraq, Iran, Greece and Rome doing on the Temple Mount? Probably they were signing the Peace Treaty of Daniel 9:27. This historic document would divide Jerusalem and allow the Israelis to rebuild the Temple. According to Daniel 9:27, once the Peace Treaty was signed, the seven year Tribulation would commence.

From The Hidden

FINAL EDITION

MMXIII   UNITED STATES OF AMERICA   SECTION I

Millions Disappear

DAMASCUS
Destroyed

ISRAEL

Is The End Here?

Wars Worldwide

Anne T. Garcia

CHAPTER 1

THE GREAT WEEK
OF
HUMAN HISTORY

The universe is approximately 14 billion years old. This is a fact upon which scientists and the Jewish sages generally agree.[1] Somewhere in those past ages ancient animals roamed, urban populations flourished, and then a cataclysmic event occurred.

This is clearly recorded in this Biblical record, in verse 2.

> [1] *In the beginning God created the heavens and the earth.* [2] *The earth was **without form, and void;** and darkness was on the face of the deep. And the Spirit of God was hovering over the face of the waters.*

³ *Then God said, "Let there be light"; and there was light.*

Genesis 1:1-3 (emphasis added)

Notice in verse 2 that darkness covered everything. God took the prophet Jeremiah backwards in time and showed him this dismal scene. Many scholars believe verse 2 refers to the destruction of a pre-Adamic civilization, which resulted from Satan's rebellion against God. Here is the way Jeremiah recorded it:

²³ *I beheld the earth, and indeed it was **without form, and void;***
And the heavens, they had no light.
²⁴ *I beheld the mountains, and indeed they trembled,*
And all the hills moved back and forth.
²⁵ *I beheld, and indeed there was no man,*
And all the birds of the heavens had fled.
²⁶ *I beheld, and indeed the fruitful land was a wilderness,*
And all its cities were broken down
At the presence of the Lord,
By His fierce anger.
²⁷ *For thus says the Lord:*

"The whole land shall be desolate;
Yet I will not make a full end.
²⁸ *For this shall the earth mourn,*
And the heavens above be black,
Because I have spoken.
I have purposed and will not relent,
Nor will I turn back from it.

Jeremiah 4:23-28 (emphasis added)

The blackness persisted throughout eons of ages until God's appointed time. And then, when it pleased Him, He gave the command in Genesis 1:3, "Let there be light" and the Light of the World came on the scene. Notice in Genesis 1:14-18 the creation of the sun, moon and stars did not occur until the fourth day. The light that came forth on the first day was the Light of the World, the Lord Jesus Christ:

> [1] *In the beginning was the Word, and the Word was with God, and the Word was God.* [2] *He was in the beginning with God.* [3] *All things were made through Him, and without Him nothing was made that was made.* [4] *In Him was life, and the life **was the light of men*** [5] *And **the light shines in the darkness,** and the darkness did not comprehend it.*
>
> John 1:1-5 (emphasis added)

And so, 6,000 years ago God created Adam and gave him dominion and a mandate to rule. We know the story all too well. Let us summarize human history from Adam to this present day:

From Adam to Abraham 2,000 years – Age of Conscience.

From Abraham to Christ 2,000 years – Age of the Law.

From Christ to the present 2,000 years – Age of Grace.

Human history has one more age to enjoy, namely the Millennial (1,000 year) Reign of Jesus Christ, before eternity begins.

I like the way Kenneth Copeland puts it: "For all practical purposes, 2,000 years have come and gone since Jesus' birth and ministry. Six thousand years since Adam was created. You and I are being squeezed between 6,000 years of time behind us and another 1,000 years ahead of us. The 1,000 years facing us is the Millennial reign of Jesus of Nazareth". [2]

And this, dear readers, is what is known as "The Great Week of Human History". But you may consider a week to be a span of time that covers seven days, while I am speaking here of a span of time that covers 7,000 years. A single verse of Scripture can quickly erase all confusion.

> _⁸ But, beloved, do not forget this one thing, that with the Lord one day is as a thousand years, and a thousand years as one day._
>
> 2 Peter 3:8

One of the purposes of the seven-day creation story was to prefigure the 7,000 years of human history. God is always working toward perfection. We know that in Hebrew, seven is the number of perfection (or completion).

Furthermore, God as much as told Isaiah that the creation story told the whole story:

> _⁹ Remember the former things of old,_
> _For I am God, and there is no other;_
> _I am God, and there is none like Me,_
> _¹⁰ **Declaring the end from the beginning...**_
>
> Isaiah 46:9-10 (emphasis added)

Yahweh said something very similar through King Solomon, the wisest man who ever lived:

> _⁹ **That which has been is what will be,**_
> _That which is done is what will be done, And there is nothing new under the sun._
> _¹⁰ **Is there anything of which it may be said, "See, this is new?"**_
> _It has already been in ancient times before us._
>
> Ecclesiastes 1:9-10 (emphasis added)

Let me use an example to illustrate this point. The first Jewish war recorded in Genesis 14, has Abram the

Hebrew battling the kings of Babylon (Shinar) and Persia. The final Jewish war, Armageddon, has Jesus, the King of the Jews again battling, and defeating Antichrist, the King of Babylon (Jeremiah 25:26; Isaiah 14:4).

Thus we have events in the Bible playing out, all the while prefiguring future events, which God desires that we delve into and understand.

This chart illustrates what we refer to as **The Great Week of Human History** :

 1 Day = 1,000 Years

2 Peter 3:8

The Great Week of Human History

Age of Conscience	Age of the Law	Age of Grace	Millennial Reign	Eternity
Days 1 and 2	3 and 4	5 and 6	7	8
2,000 Years	2,000 Years	2,000 Years	1,000 Years	
Adam	Abraham	Jesus	Now	Great White Throne Judgment

Using this chart, we see a total of seven days, which we understand from 2 Peter 3:8 to be 7,000 years. Adam was created at the beginning of day one, and after the fall of man he had to find God's will by using his conscience. Thus, we have the first 2,000 year period called the "Age of Conscience". Unfortunately, man did not do a very good job of living by his conscience, because 1,700 years into human history God, who is love, sent the flood.

LOVE SENT THE FLOOD

Love sent the flood? Yes, dear reader, you and I would not be here today if God had not sent the flood. Mankind was deteriorating into sinfulness so rapidly that soon all men would have been hell bound. In Genesis 11 right after the flood, we see Nimrod building the Tower of Babel, again defying God. God had to do something! And so, five generations later He raised up Abraham and gave man a better way to righteousness.

The "Age of the Law" began when God cut covenant with Abraham in Genesis 15. On Mount Sinai the Law came into fullness when Moses was given the Ten Commandments. The "Age of the Law" was fulfilled with the ministry of the Lord Jesus, who was born about 3 B.C.

The "Age of Grace" was introduced at the Last Supper:

> ^{26} *And as they were eating, Jesus took bread, blessed and broke it, and gave it to the disciples and said, "Take, eat; this is My body".*
> ^{27} *Then He took the cup, and gave thanks, and gave it to them, saying, "Drink from it, all of you.* ^{28} *For this is My blood of **the new covenant**, which is shed for many for the remission of sins*
> Matthew 26:26-28 (emphasis added)

It came into fullness on Pentecost Sunday:

> ^{1} *When the Day of Pentecost had fully come, they were all with one accord in one place.* ^{2} *And suddenly there came a sound from heaven, as of a rushing mighty wind, and it filled the whole house where they were sitting.* ^{3} *Then there appeared to them divided tongues, as of fire, and one sat upon each of them.* ^{4} *And they were **all filled with the Holy Spirit** and began to speak with other*

– 22 –

tongues, as the Spirit gave them utterance.
Acts 2:1-4 (emphasis added)

Today we are at the culmination of the "Age of Grace", also called the "Age of Faith" or the "Church Age".

We recall that when Moses came down the mountain with the Ten Commandments, he found the people in sin. As retribution, God required him to send the Levites among the people, executing **about three thousand** of them (Exodus 32:26-28). On Pentecost Sunday, the birth of the "Age of Grace", we see that **about three thousand** souls were added to the Church (Acts 2:41). Thus we see a great truth revealed: *"The letter kills but the Spirit gives life"* (2 Corinthians 3:6).

We should be forever grateful to the Lord for allowing us to live during the "Age of Grace". In the Bible, the "Age of Grace" is also referred to as the "Last Days". In Biblical times the Jews always referred to days by their number. Sunday was "the first day of the week", Wednesday was the "fourth day of the week", and so on. God always works toward completion or perfection, and seven is the number of completion. Thus, the Jews were always working toward the seventh day, the Sabbath, after which they would begin again.

Reviewing our chart, we see that the last two days (or 2,000 years) before the 1,000 year Sabbath rest are days five and six. Hence, the following scriptures refer to the "Church Age" as the "Last Days".

> [16] *But this is what was spoken by the prophet Joel:*
> [17] *And it shall come to pass **in the last days**, says God,*
> *That I will pour out of My Spirit on all flesh;*
> *Your sons and your daughters shall prophesy;*
> *Your young men shall see visions,*

Your old men shall dream dreams.
Acts 2:16-17 (emphasis added)

[1] *But know this, that **in the last days** perilous times will come:* [2] *For men will be lovers of themselves, lovers of money, boasters, proud, blasphemers, disobedient to parents, unthankful, unholy,...*
2 Timothy 3:1-2 (emphasis added)

[17] *But you, beloved, remember the words which were spoken before by the apostles of our Lord Jesus Christ:* [18] *how they told you that there would be mockers **in the last time** who would walk according to their own ungodly lusts.*
Jude 17-18 (emphasis added)

We are actually living at the end of the sixth, or last day. Some may ask, the last day before what? The answer is obvious: the last day before the Sabbath, or seventh day, the Millennial Age. Knowing that we are in the last day makes these words of Jesus in John so much clearer. He's telling us when the Rapture will be. We are not surprised to find out we'll be Raptured on the last day:

[40] *And this is the will of Him who sent Me, that everyone who sees the Son and believes in Him may have everlasting life; and I will raise him up at the last day.*

[44] *No one can come to Me unless the Father who sent Me draws him; and **I will raise him up at the last day**.*

[54] *Whoever eats My flesh and drinks My blood has eternal life, and **I will raise him up at the last day**.*
John 6:40, 44, 54 (emphasis added)

Sometimes the words "Last Days" and "End Times"

– 24 –

are used interchangeably, but that is incorrect. The "Last Days" began, as I have illustrated, on Pentecost. The "End Times" began, in my opinion, when the Lord's parable of the fig tree (Israel) was fulfilled and Israel became a nation again, May 14, 1948.

> [29] *Then He spoke to them a parable: "Look at the fig tree, and all the trees.* [30] *When they are already budding, you see and know for yourselves that summer is now near.* [31] *So you also, when you see these things happening, (prophecy being fullfilled) know that the kingdom of God is near.* [32] *Assuredly, I say to you, this generation will by no means pass away till all things take place.*
>
> Luke 21:29-32
>
> (parenthesis are author's interpretation)

The "End Times" will culminate in a period often referred to as "The Judgment of the Nations". Could it be that we are already in the time period known as "The Judgment of the Nations?" If so, what does the future hold for you and me?

Notice in verse 30 Jesus says, *"you see and know for yourself that summer is now near"*. When is summer? It is the time when Jesus returns to judge the goat nations.

> [35] *"Then the iron, the clay, the bronze, the silver, and the gold were crushed together, and became like chaff from the <u>summer</u> threshing floors;"*
>
> Daniel 2:35a

CHAPTER 2

THE JUDGMENT
OF
THE NATIONS

The Judgment of the Nations is a time in history when nations will finally reap what they have sown. I recall giving counsel to my children many times as they were growing up: "No one ever gets away with anything". So it is with the nations. At the end of the Tribulation, all judgment on this earth will be reduced to this question, "How did you treat Israel and the Jews?" (Matthew 25:31-46).

Many Christian and Jewish scholars believe the Judgment of the Nations began on Rosh Hashanah in the year right after 1998, the year the Jews celebrated 50 years in the land. That is, the Judgment of the Nations began on September 11, 1999.[3]

If this is accurate, it could explain why Satan chose September 11, 2001 as the date to attack the United States, sort of a return salvo from the powers of darkness.

In any event, I believe we are living in that judgment time, which is characterized by:

1. All previously unfulfilled prophetic wars will occur. These wars include:

The Iraqi Wars	Jeremiah 50, 51
The leveling of Damascus	Isaiah 17
The war of Gog and Magog	Ezekiel 38, 39
Armageddon	Revelation 19:11-21 and Zechariah 12 & 14

This knowledge **should not strike terror** in the heart of the reader. Just the opposite, really. We are living in the most exciting time of history, with an unparalleled opportunity before us. We are not here by accident. God put us here at this time because He knew that by His grace we would get the job done! What job? The job of harvesting the seed sown by the sacrifice of the martyrs, the tears of the missionaries and the prayers of mothers and fathers on their knees for the past 2,000 years! If we will stay faithful to our call, and many of us will, we will forever reign as *"kings and priests to our God; And we shall reign on the earth. (Revelation 5:10)"*.

2. Judgments will become more rapid in succession and more severe.

> [7] *For nation will rise against nation, and kingdom against kingdom. And there will be famines, pestilences, and earthquakes in various places.*
>
> Matthew 24:7

3. God, who is love, will use these catastrophes and judgments to draw men to Himself.

> [9] *...For when Your judgments are in the earth, The inhabitants of the world will learn righteousness.*
>
> Isaiah 26:9

He will increase His glory during judgment.

> [21] *I will set My glory among the nations; all the nations shall see My judgment which I have executed, and My hand which I have laid on them.*
>
> Ezekiel 39:21

4. The time will finally come when the sin-laden nations will be weary and the glory will be full:

> [13] *Behold, is it not of the Lord of hosts*
> *That the peoples labor to feed the fire,*
> *And nations weary themselves in vain?*
> [14] *For the earth will be filled*
> *With the knowledge of the glory of the Lord,*
> *As the waters cover the sea.*
>
> Habakkuk 2:13-14

5. Then the Bride of Christ, the Church, will be Raptured, as prophesied by Hosea: (remember that the Age of Grace lasts 2,000 years, or "two days.).

> [2] *After two days He will revive us;*

On the third day He will raise us up,
That we may live in His sight.

Hosea 6:2

After the Rapture, Jesus will receive us, the Bride of Christ, at the heavenly wedding feast. We see a confirmation of the timing of this wedding feast cleverly woven into the fabric of the gospel of John:

[1] On the third day, there was a wedding…

John 2:1

This refers to the third day (1,000 years) of Christianity.

As we stated above, God always desires man to repent. Notice that even during the second half of the Tribulation, God sends angels to be seen by men, with warnings not to be ignored.

> *[6] Then I saw another angel flying in the midst of heaven, having the everlasting gospel to preach to those who dwell on the earth—to every nation, tribe, tongue, and people— [7] saying with a loud voice, "Fear God and give glory to Him, for the hour of His judgment has come; and worship Him who made heaven and earth, the sea and springs of water".*
>
> *[9] Then a third angel followed them, saying with a loud voice, **"If anyone worships the beast and his image, and receives his mark on his forehead or on his hand,** [10] he himself shall also drink of the wine of the wrath of God, which is poured out full strength into the cup of His indignation. He shall be tormented with fire and brimstone in the presence of the holy angels and in the presence of the Lamb".*

Revelation 14:6-7, 9-10 (emphasis added)

And finally, right before the battle called "Armageddon" (actually the battle for Jerusalem), the Lord Himself, filled with love for His rebellious children, makes one last appeal:

> [15] *"Behold, I am coming as a thief. Blessed is he who watches, and keeps his garments, lest he walk naked and they see his shame."*
>
> [16] *And they gathered them together to the place called in Hebrew, Armageddon.*
>
> Revelation 16:15-16

As on earth, a court must be assembled in heaven, with a presiding judge, before a judgment can be pronounced. The world will have its day in court, as illustrated in both the Old and New Testaments: (Please refer to full page chart on page 32.)

PARALLEL VERSES IN DANIEL AND REVELATION

Daniel 7:9a 9 I watched till thrones were put in place, And the Ancient of Days was seated; His garment was white as snow, And the hair of his head was like pure wool.	Revelation 4:2, 3, 4 2 Immediately I was in the spirit; and behold a throne set in heaven, and One sat on the throne... 3 And He who sat there was like jasper and sardius stone... 4 Around the throne were twenty-four thrones, and on the thrones I saw twenty-four elders sitting, clothed in white robes; and they had crowns of gold on their heads.
Daniel 7:10a 10 A fiery stream issued And came forth from before Him, A thousand thousands ministered to Him; Ten thousand times ten thousand stood before Him.	Revelation 5:11, 12 11 Then I looked, and I heard the voice of many angels around the throne, the living creatures, and the elders; and the number of them was ten thousand times ten thousand, and thousands of thousands, 12 saying with a loud voice: Worthy is the Lamb who was slain.
Daniel 7:10b ... The court was seated, And the books were opened.	Revelation 5:5 5 But one of the elders said to me, "Do not weep. Behold, the Lion of the tribe of Judah, the Root of David, has prevailed to open the scroll and to loose its seven seals."
Daniel 7:14 14 Then to Him was given dominion and glory and a kingdom, That all peoples, nations, and languages should serve Him. His dominion is an everlasting dominion, Which shall not pass away, And His kingdom the one Which shall not be destroyed.	Revelation 11:15 15 Then the seventh angel sounded: And there were loud voices in heaven, saying, "The kingdoms of this world have become the kingdoms of our Lord and of His Christ, and He shall reign forever and ever!"

A review of the characteristics of the time of the Judgment of the Nations reveals that all Biblical wars will be completed, judgments will be progressively harsher and more proximate, and God's hand of mercy will be extended throughout. Glory will fill the church, and then it will be taken out.

Let us look again at the King James Version of Daniel 7:10:

> [10]...*the judgment was set, and the books were opened.*

I believe the judgment was set on September 11, 1999 (see page 28). In the Bible, a punctuation mark can represent an extended period of time. I believe that we are living in a time represented by the comma after the word "set". We will continue in this time frame until after the Rapture of the Church. At that time the "books will be opened". "And the books were opened" is discussed in greater detail in Chapter 4.

The chart on the following page gives an analysis of what I believe will transpire during the time of the Judgment of the Nations. There is no unanimity of opinion among Bible teachers on the sequence of the events. I invite the readers to search the Scripture and see what the Holy Spirit reveals to their own hearts.

Some scholars believe the leveling of Damascus will be the event that triggers the war of Ezekiel 38 and 39. I agree with that view for four reasons:

1. Syria, an arch foe of Israel, does not take part in the attack against Israel in Ezekiel 38 and 39.

2. Two powerful eschatological portions of Scripture, the book of Amos and Zechariah 9, begin with the destruction of Damascus.

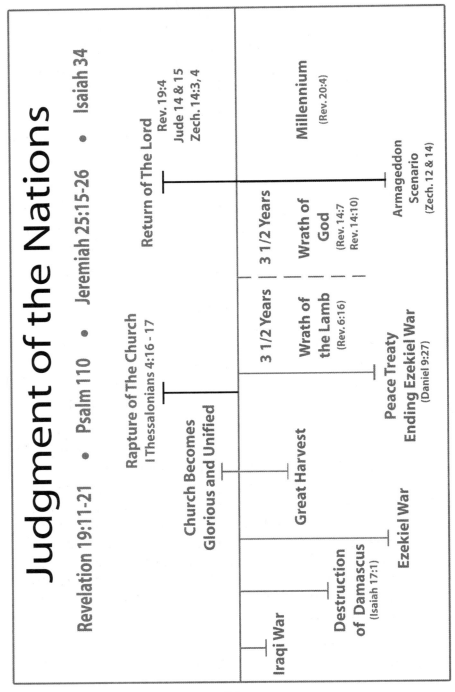

Judgment of the Nations

Revelation 19:11-21 • Psalm 110 • Jeremiah 25:15-26 • Isaiah 34

Iraqi War

Destruction
of Damascus
(Isaiah 17:1)

Ezekiel War

Church Becomes
Glorious and Unified

Great Harvest

Rapture of The Church
I Thessalonians 4:16 - 17

Peace Treaty
Ending Ezekiel War
(Daniel 9:27)

3 1/2 Years

Wrath of
the Lamb
(Rev. 6:16)

3 1/2 Years

Wrath of
God
(Rev. 14:7
Rev. 14:10)

Return of The Lord

Rev. 19:4
Jude 14 & 15
Zech. 14:3, 4

Armageddon
Scenario
(Zech. 12 & 14)

Millennium
(Rev. 20:4)

3. Isaiah 17, the chapter that prophesies "Damascus will cease from being a city", ends with three verses (12-14) that appear to be the Ezekiel war. This would imply that the destruction of Damascus precedes the Ezekiel war.

> 12 *Woe to the multitude of many people*
> *Who make a noise like the roar of the seas,*
> *And to the rushing of nations*
> *That make a rushing like the rushing of mighty waters!*
> 13 *The nations will rush like the rushing of many waters;*
> *But God will rebuke them and they will flee far away, And be chased like the chaff of the mountains before the wind,*
> *Like a rolling thing before the whirlwind.*
> 14 *Then behold, at eventide, trouble!*
> *And before the morning, he is no more. This is the portion of those who plunder us, And the lot of those who rob us.*
>
> Isaiah 17:12-14

4. Building on what I have just explained, a careful reading of Jeremiah 49:23-27 seems to prophesy a naval attack by the Israelis leading to a fire in Damascus, no doubt a very powerful bomb. (Amos 1:4 confirms that fire will devour Damascus.) I have emphasized verse 25. We see the prophet Jeremiah implying this in verse 25: The Syrians are attacking us. We must either destroy Damascus or evacuate Jerusalem. We choose, therefore, to destroy Damascus. (Jerusalem, of course is the city of God's joy.)

> 23 *Against Damascus.*
> *"Hamath and Arpad are shamed,*

> *For they have heard bad news.*
> *They are fainthearted; There is trouble on the sea;*
> *It cannot be quiet.*
> ²⁴ *Damascus has grown feeble;*
> *She turns to flee*
> *And fear has seized her.*
> *Anguish and sorrows have taken her like a woman*
> *in labor.*
> ²⁵ **Why is the city of praise not deserted, the**
> **city of My joy?**
> ²⁶ *Therefore her young men shall fall in her streets,*
> *And all the men of war shall be cut off in that*
> *day", says the Lord of hosts.*
> ²⁷ *"I will kindle a fire in the wall of Damascus, And*
> *it shall consume the palaces of Ben-Hadad".*
> Jeremiah 49:23-27 (emphasis added)

I will discuss the Ezekiel war in detail in Chapter 6. It is pivotal to understanding the direction to which each of the four horsemen will travel.

The first of the four horsemen, the man on the white horse, we believe will be the Antichrist. Some authors have opined the first rider is Jesus. This cannot be. Jesus is in heaven opening the seals, not riding the white horse on earth.

It is worth noting that the first mention of the Antichrist is in Isaiah 10:5 where he is called the Assyrian. The "first mention" of any subject in the Bible is significant. The first mention is its overarching definition. All further mentions will expand on and agree with the first mention.

Furthermore, Scripture teaches that he will be revealed after the Rapture.

> ⁷ *For the mystery of lawlessness is already at work;*

only He who now restrains will do so until He is taken out of the way. 8 And then the lawless one will be revealed, whom the Lord will consume with the breath of His mouth and destroy with the brightness of His coming.

2 Thessalonians 2:7-8

Who is "He" who restrains the Antichrist, forbidding him from being revealed? He is the Body of Christ. Now we know that the Body of Christ is sometimes referred to in the feminine as the "Bride of Christ". The Body of Christ is also referred to sometimes in the masculine:

*13 till we all come to the unity of the faith and of the knowledge of the Son of God, to a **perfect man**, to the measure of the stature of the fullness of Christ;*

Ephesians 4:13 (emphasis added)

Therefore, "He" who restrains the Antichrist from being revealed is none other than the "perfect man" of Ephesians 4:13. Namely, "He" is the Body of Christ. It is my view that as we pray for the "peace" of Jerusalem, we pray that there will be "nothing missing, nothing broken" in Jerusalem. Evil men will not be able to divide this Holy City until the Church is removed from the earth in the Rapture. After we leave, the peace treaty of Daniel 9:27 will be signed, followed immediately by the Tribulation.

Let me outline a series of events, which I believe will soon transpire on the earth.

1. Syria will attack Israel.

2. Israel will counterattack by sea to save Jerusalem, leveling Damascus.

3. Indignation in Russia and the Muslim community will precipitate the Ezekiel War.

4. God will defeat the Russian and Muslim invaders on the mountains of Israel (see Chapter 6).

5. After the Rapture, a diplomat will come from Syria to Jerusalem to broker a seven year peace treaty with Israel. This diplomat is the Antichrist:

²⁷ *Then he shall confirm a covenant with many for one week; But in the middle of the week he shall bring an end to sacrifice and offering. And on the wing of abominations shall be one who makes desolate, Even until the consummation, which is determined, Is poured out on the desolate.*

Daniel 9:27

Let us read on to see what else the Scripture has to say about this diabolical man.

CHAPTER 3

THE ANTICHRIST PERSONA

Before I attempt to identify the four horsemen, we must understand where the Antichrist comes from since he rides on one of the horses. He is identified in Revelation 13:1 as a beast with seven heads. Those **seven heads** represent the kingdoms that have come against national Israel throughout history.

Egypt		
Assyria		
Babylon............... **Lion**		
Medo-Persia.......... **Bear**	**Daniel 7:4 - 8**	
Greece................. **Leopard**	**"Four Great Beasts"**	
Rome.................. **Dreadful Beast**		
Revived Rome		

The vision of the four beasts in Daniel 7 identifies the four world powers that dominated ancient Jerusalem, described as beasts.

A comparison of the beasts in Daniel 7:4-8 and the description of Antichrist in Revelation is striking:

> [2] *Now the beast which I saw was like a **leopard**, his feet were like the feet of a **bear**, and his mouth like the mouth of a **lion**. The dragon gave him his power, his throne, and great authority.*
>
> Revelation 13:2 (emphasis added)

I render this description to infer: Now the Antichrist was like a Greek (**leopard**), his feet walked where the Medo-Persians (**bear**) walked, and his mouth devoured what the Babylonians (**lion**) devoured.

Thus I conclude that the Antichrist will be of Greek origin, take over Iraq as the Medo-Persians did and subsequently "devour" Jerusalem as the Babylonians did. In fact, the Antichrist is referred to as the King of Babylon (Isaiah 14:4) and the King of Sheshach (Jeremiah 25:26). Sheshach is a code name for Babylon. The Antichrist is also called the Assyrian (Isaiah 10:24 and 14:25 and Micah 5:5,6).

In fact the first mention of the Antichrist in the Bible is in Isaiah 10:5. He is called the "Assyrian". The Biblical "law of first mention" says this. The first time any topic is mentioned in the Word is its overarching definition. All future references will agree with and/or expand on the first mention.

One of the types for the coming Antichrist was the Pharoah who Moses defeated. He was not an Egyptian. He was an Assyrian. Isaiah 52:4 says, For thus says the Lord God: "My people went down at first Into Egypt to dwell there; Then the Assyrian oppressed them without cause".

In Daniel we see the Antichrist introduced as the "little horn", that comes up from among the ten horns, or ten kingdoms of the end times.

> [7] *After this I saw in the night visions, and behold, a fourth beast, dreadful and terrible, exceedingly strong. It had huge iron teeth; it was devouring, breaking in pieces, and trampling the residue with its feet. It was different from all the beasts that were before it, and it had ten horns.* [8] *I was considering the horns, and there was **another horn, a little one**, coming up among them, before whom three of the first horns were plucked out by the roots. And there, in this horn, are eyes like the eyes of a man, and a mouth speaking pompous words.*
>
> Daniel 7:7-8 (emphasis added)

We don't have to try to interpret these verses, since someone who saw the vision with Daniel, probably an angel, gives the interpretation.

> [23] *Thus he said:*
> *The fourth beast shall be*
> *A fourth kingdom on earth,*
> *Which shall be different from all other kingdoms,*
> *and shall devour the whole earth,*
> *Trample it and break it in pieces.*
> [24] *The ten horns are ten kings*
> *Who shall arise from this kingdom.*
> *And **another shall rise after them;***
> ***He shall be different from the first ones,***
> ***And shall subdue three kings.***
> [25] *He shall speak pompous words against the Most High,*
> *Shall persecute the saints of the Most High,*
> *And shall intend to change times and law.*

> *Then the saints shall be given into his hand*
> *For a time and times and half a time.*
> Daniel 7:23-25 (emphasis added)

Agreeing with Daniel 7:24, Daniel 8 narrows down the focus of who the little horn could be:

> [8] *Therefore the male goat grew very great; but when he became strong, the large horn was broken, and in place of it four notable ones came up toward the four winds of heaven.* [9] ***And out of one of them came a little horn,*** *which grew exceedingly great toward the south, toward the east, and toward the Glorious Land.*
> Daniel 8:8-9 (emphasis added)

We are grateful to the Angel Gabriel, who interpreted the vision for Daniel.

> [21] *And the male goat is the kingdom of Greece. The large horn that is between its eyes is the first king.* [22] *As for the broken horn and the four that stood up in its place, four kingdoms shall arise out of that nation, but not with its power.* [23] *And* ***in the latter time of their kingdom, When the transgressors have reached their fullness,*** *A king shall arise, having fierce features, who understands sinister schemes.* [24] *His power shall be mighty, but not by his own power; He shall destroy fearfully, And shall prosper and thrive; He shall destroy the mighty, and also the holy people.*
> Daniel 8:21-24 (emphasis added)

Thus, we see that the little horn, the Antichrist, must arise out of one of the four divisions of Alexander's Greek empire.

A careful rendering of ancient Greek history shows that the "first king", Alexander the Great, died in 323 B.C. At that time, his kingdom was divided between four generals. They are the four kingdoms referred to in Daniel 8:22.

GENERAL	TOOK	GEOGRAPHICAL AREA
General Cassander	—	Greece
General Lysimachus	—	Turkey
General Seleucus	—	Syria & Iraq
General Ptlolemy	—	Egypt

The next verse, Daniel 8:23, makes it clear that the Antichrist will arise from one of these four kingdoms. It's important to note that all four generals were Greek by nationality, as stated in Daniel 8:22 (remember the Antichrist must be of Greek national origin to satisfy Revelation 13:2 and Zechariah 9:13).

Antichrist is also called the "Assyrian" and the "King of Babylon". So let us take a closer look at General Seleucus, who ruled out of Antioch, Syria. Assyria included Syria, Southern Turkey, and Iraq; the borders were very fluid. Babylon conquered Assyria in 612 B.C. The combination of Babylon and Assyria is known as the "Fertile Crescent".

It is believed by many that the "Fertile Crescent" will be the power base of the future Antichrist. Political events in the Middle East have caused increased Shia /Sunni friction. It is my view that the Antichrist will represent the Shiite branch of Islam. Refer to the chart below to see why the Antichrist will represent Shiites.

Why Antichrist Represents Shiites

1. Iran, the most dangerous nation in the world is Shiite, and has vowed to rule the world.

2. Antichrist is called the "King of Babylon," (Isaiah 14:4) a Shiite city in Iraq.

3. Babylon is where all false religion began, and will be the future world economic center during the Great Tribulation (Zechariah 5:5-11; Revelation 18).

4. The Sunni want to rule from the Levant, which will be depopulated, possibly due to radiation (Isaiah 17:1-2 and Joel 3:19).

5. The doctrine of the "Mahdi" (promised one/antichrist) originated with the Shiites, the so-called "Twelvers".

6. The antichrist ascends to power after destroying Egypt, a leading Sunni nation (Daniel 11:42, 43).

It appears we are looking for a man of Greek national origin, whose citizenship is in Syria, and will be called the "King of the North", (Daniel 11:40) who will one day seize Jerusalem as his base, and set an idol in the holy place.

Has there ever been such an evil person on the face of the earth? The answer is "yes", the Seleucid king, Antiochus IV Epiphanes. King Antiochus Epiphanes was a ruthless Greek ruler from Syria who was determined to totally subjugate Jewish culture. Greek language and customs were thrust upon the Jews, and worship of Zeus the Greek god was mandated. Antiochus IV ruled from 175 B.C. to 164 B.C. Fierce resistance by the Jews, rallied by a great warrior named Judas Maccabee, characterized the last three years of his reign. Jewish scholars see the Jewish military victory over Antiochus Epiphanes in 164 B.C. as a fulfillment of this prophecy written 300 years before the war.

> [13] *For I have bent Judah, My bow,*
> *Fitted the bow with Ephraim,*
> *And raised up your sons, O Zion,*
> *Against your sons, O Greece,*
> *And made you like the sword of a mighty man.*
>
> Zechariah 9:13

However, David Baron states emphatically "the prophecy cannot be altogether restricted to the Maccabean struggle with the Syrian Greeks". David Baron was born in Russia in 1855 and raised in the best Rabbinical schools of Europe. He found Jesus to be Messiah while studying the Old Testament. His prolific writings were addressed to Jews and Christians alike. He goes on to explain:

> *No; Zion and Greece, as has been well observed by another writer, are in this prophecy of Zechariah opposed to one another as the city of God and the city of the world (the civitas Dei, and the civitas mundi, as Augustine has it), and the defeat of Antiochus Epiphanes and his successors at the hands of comparative handfuls of despised Jews, to which this passage may primarily refer, **foreshadows***

the final conflict with world-power, and the judgments to be inflicted on the confederated armies who shall be gathered against Jerusalem, not only directly by the hand of God, but also by the hand of Israel, who shall then be made strong in Jehovah. (emphasis added)[4]

Thus we see the defeat of Antiochus Epiphanes by Judas Maccabee prefigures the defeat of Antichrist by the Lord Jesus Christ.

The comparison in the chart on the next page between Antiochus Epiphanes and the coming Antichrist includes many chilling facts:

	ANTIOCHUS	ANTICHRIST
1. Both have Greek ancestors	Daniel 8:22	Daniel 8:23
2a. Outlaws the solemn feasts	2 Maccabees 6:6	--------------------
2b. Attempts to outlaw the feasts	--------------------	Daniel 7:25
3. Takes away daily sacrifice	Daniel 11:31	Daniel 9:7
4. Defiles the temple of God	2 Maccabees 6:1	Daniel 9:27
5a. Compels the people to worship the god Baccus or be put to death	2 Maccabees 6:7-9	--------------------
5b. Compels the people to worship the beast, his image, or be put to death	--------------------	Revelation 13:15-17
6. Jews will suffer under his reign	2 Maccabees 6:16	Daniel 2:44 Daniel 7:25-26
7. Sets up the idol of abomination of desolation on the altar of God	1 Maccabees 1:57 Daniel 11:31	Mark 13:14 Daniel 12:11
8. Challenged by the Roman Empire	Daniel 11:30	Revelation 17
9. Attacks and defeats Egypt	Daniel 11:25	Daniel 11:40, 42-43
10. An extended peace follows his overthrow.	Peace from 163 B.C. to 63 B.C.	Revelation 20:4 (Jesus reigns for 1,000 years)

One of the notable differences between Antiochus Epiphanes and the Antichrist has to do with religious beliefs. Antiochus Epiphanes was a pagan, while the Antichrist will worship a *"god of forces"* (Daniel 11:38). Islam has always conquered by military force. Many modern scholars believe Antichrist will be a Muslim military and/or political leader.

The Shiite Muslim doctrine of the "Mahdi" (Guided One or Hidden Imam) teaches that the twelfth prophet (descendant of Ali) disappeared in the desert in the 800's. Called a "sinless and absolutely infallible" holy man, he will come from the desert at the end of days on a white horse to unite the world under Islam.[5]

It is interesting to note that the Shiite branch of the Islamic faith is on the rise, particularly among the young and impoverished in Muslim countries. Mohammad's command to his followers before his death was: "Fight until all declare, there is no god but Allah".

Could that command be the driving force behind the war of terror that is currently being waged against us?

Before we leave the Antichrist model, let us refer the reader back to #7 in the chart on page 47. We will examine the term "abomination of desolation" in light of the Book of Maccabees. (Maccabees is considered historical, but not part of Scripture, except by the Catholic Church.)

Daniel warns of the future abomination of desolation:

> [11] *And from the time that the daily sacrifice is taken away, and the abomination of desolation is set up, there shall be one thousand two hundred and ninety days.*
>
> Daniel 12:11

Jesus affirms the accuracy of Daniel's prophecy in Mark 13:14: *"So when you see the 'abomination of desolation,' spoken of by Daniel the prophet, standing where it ought not"* — (let the reader understand) — *"then let those who are in Judea flee to the mountains".* And so we ask the question, what is the *"abomination of desolation?"* In the light of the Book of Maccabees, we understand that they are referring to an idol called in the Book of Revelation the *"image of the beast"*. King Antiochus set up as an idol, a statue of Jupiter, on the altar:

> ^{57} *On the fifteenth day of the month Casleu, in the hundred and forty-fifth year, king Antiochus set up the abominable idol of desolation upon the altar of God,...*
>
> I Maccabees 1: 57 (DRA))

We know from the Word of God that the false prophet will set up an image of the beast.

> ^{14} *And he deceives those who dwell on the earth by those signs which he was granted to do in the sight of the beast, telling those who dwell on the earth to make an image to the beast who was wounded by the sword and lived.* ^{15} *He was granted power to give breath to the image of the beast, that the image of the beast should both speak and* **cause as many as would not worship the image of the beast to be killed.**
>
> Revelation 13:14-15 (emphasis added)

In conclusion let us re-examine two important facts:

1. The Muslims are waiting for an Islamic leader to ride out of the desert and take over the world.

2. Half way through the Tribulation Period, (Revelation 13:14, 15), Antichrist will set up the image of the beast inside the Temple Holy Place. Consider the warning of Jesus to those who will be alive during the Tribulation Period, in light of these two facts:

^{25} *See, I have told you beforehand.*
^{26} *"Therefore if they say to you, 'Look, **He is in the desert!**' do not go out; or 'Look, **He is in the inner rooms!**' do not believe it.*

Matthew 24:25-26 (emphasis added)

It is my view that the Lord is referring in this Scripture to the Muslim world leader, *"He is in the desert"*, and the image of the beast, *"He is in the inner rooms"* (we will look at the beast and his image in greater detail in Chapter 13).

As I stated in Chapter 2 of this book, the Judgment of the Nations began on September 11, 1999. What is the one thing holding back the four horsemen of the Apocalypse? The books have not been opened.

^{10} *...the judgment was set, and the books were opened.*

Daniel 7:10 (KJV)

When the books are opened, the four horsemen will be released. But who will open the books?

CHAPTER 4

THE FOUR HORSEMEN DEFINED

The entire fifth chapter of the Book of Revelation is the story of who will open the book. (Although the New King James Version calls it a scroll, that is incorrect. "Scroll" is a correct translation of Revelation 6:1, but not a correct translation of the book in Revelation 5. <u>Strong's Concordance</u> calls the "book" biblion, a diminutive of biblos, from which we get the word Bible.) A frantic search is made in heaven, then on earth, and finally, even in hell to find someone who is worthy to open the book (Revelation 5:3). No one is found. John feels so helpless, he weeps much (Revelation 5:4). Why would John weep? Most scholars see the book as the title deed to planet earth. He knows the book must be opened, in order to conclude the time of judgment. After the judgment, the Messiah will reign, and John's beloved country, Israel, will be returned to its rightful place. It will be the center of all earthly business, the ruling kingdom of the world. The Millennial Temple will be built; and there will be "heaven on earth". Like any good Jew, he longs for this day.

Suddenly, standing before John, is "the Lamb that was slain". What joy! What ecstasy! Worship and praise follow. And then Jesus walks up to His Father, takes the book, and begins to break the seals.

Thus, the book is opened.   Revelation 6 reveals that when the first four seals of the book are broken by Jesus, riders come riding on horses: white, red, black and green. The King James Version of the Bible refers to the fourth horse as the pale horse. However, the actual word in Greek translates as green.   Much speculation has gone forth throughout the ages on this topic. Who are those riders, where are they going, and for what purpose? As stated in the Introduction of this book the four horsemen are seen as: Antichrist, war, famine and "death and hell". We will not disagree wit those traditional definitions. Rather we will expand on them by noting that they are further explained as the four chariots in Zechariah 6.

WHO ARE THOSE RIDERS
AND WHERE ARE THEY GOING?

Let us begin by answering these questions. Who are the four horsemen, where are they going, and for what purpose? As background we need to understand that there are four nations who abuse Israel and the Jews during the times of the Gentiles.

The times of the gentiles began in 606 B.C. when Nebuchadnezzar attacked Jerusalem and will conclude when Jesus returns at the end of the Tribulation.

[24] *...and Jerusalem shall be trodden down of the Gentiles, until the times of the Gentiles be fulfilled.*

Luke 21:24b

The chief nations opposing Israel are given in detail for the first time in the Book of Daniel.

COUNTRY	NEBUCHADNEZZAR'S IMAGE (DANIEL 2)	FOUR GREAT BEASTS (DANIEL 7)	RAM & THE GOAT (DANIEL 8)
Babylon (Iraq)	Head — Gold —	Lion	
Medo-Persia (Iran)	Chest and Arms — Silver —	Bear	Ram
Greece	Belly and Thighs — Bronze —	Leopard	Goat
Rome — — — Revived Rome	Legs — Iron — — — — — Feet and Toes — Iron and Clay —	Dreadful Beast	

Let us take a moment to reflect on these four kingdoms in modern times: Babylon is Iraq, Medo-Persia is Iran, Graeco-Macedonia is Greece, the Roman Empire is the European Union and the Arab states.

1. Iraq - Iraq is now firmly under the control of Iran. President Obama chose to pull out all American troops after he took over as president. Recently, the U.S. requested that Iraq cease from allowing Iran to use its air space to rearm Syria. Iraq declined to cooperate. It is now a client state of Iran.

2. Iran - It appears the Ayatollahs of Iran will be the "Hitlers" of the third and final World War. They are rearmed to the teeth, and soon to be nuclear. Inexplicitly (as of this moment) the United States and Israel have failed to shut them down. Time is running out.

3. Greece - Greece appears to be an insignificant, bankrupt country, but Scripture indicates it will be an end time player.

[21]And the male goat is the kingdom of Greece. The large horn that is between its eyes is the first king.

[22]As for the broken horn and the four that stood up in its place, four kingdoms shall arise out of that nation, but not with its power.

[23]And in the latter time of their kingdom, When the transgressors have reached their fullness, A king shall arise, Having fierce features, Who understands sinister schemes".

Daniel 8:21-23

Before we continue on to the next kingdom, let's first look at some interesting facts about Greece - see the chart on the next page.

Facts About Greece

1. Greece is the only NATO member state that has strong traditional military ties with Russia. The armies of both countries are co-operating and co-training together on a regular basis. The Russian landing Ship "Novacherkassak" of the Black Sea Fleet joined the 2012 national parades in the Greek cities of Thessalonica and Lemnos. (Wikipedia)

2. Greece is bankrupt. Russia has offered to pay Greek debt. So far, Greece has declined the offer.

3. Greece is less than 1% Islamic. However, they recently authorized their government to spend 1 million Euros to build the first mosque in Athens.

4. Russia is a major supplier of oil and gas to Greece. The two nations are attempting to build a pipeline through Greece together.

5. 2013/2014 has been declared: "The year of Greece in Russia, the year of Russia in Greece."

6. Daniel Chapters 7 & 8 and Zechariah Chapter 9 prophesy toward a Greek presence in the End Times.

---

4. Revived Rome - Look for the European Union to continue its alliance with the Arab states of the Middle East and North Africa. Together, they make up the "Union for the Mediterranean", which I believe will be the future Revived Roman Empire.

Now that we have identified the four nations who abused Israel and the Jews in the Book of Daniel, we ask ourselves this question. **Are these same four nations in the Book of Zechariah?**

Zechariah was visited with eight visions in one night.

(These visions are the subject of Zechariah 1-6). The eight visions lay out the future of the Jews from Zechariah's time to the coming of Messiah in glory.

Zechariah's eighth vision is of the four chariots. **The four chariots appear to be a parallel for the four horsemen**.

Let us now examine the vision of the four chariots of Zechariah 6.

> *[1] Then I turned and raised my eyes and looked, and behold, four chariots were coming from between two mountains, and the mountains were mountains of bronze. [2] With the first chariot were red horses, with the second chariot black horses, [3] with the third chariot white horses, and with the fourth chariot dappled horses—strong steeds. [4] Then I answered and said to the angel who talked with me, "What are these, my lord?"*
> *[5] And the angel answered and said to me, "These are four spirits of heaven, who go out from their station before the Lord of all the earth. [6] The one with the black horses is going to the north country, the white are going after them, and the dappled are going toward the south country." [7] Then the strong steeds went out, eager to go, that they might walk to and fro throughout the earth. And He said, "Go, walk to and fro throughout the earth." So they walked to and fro throughout the earth. [8] And He called to me, and spoke to me, saying, "See, those who go toward the north country have given rest to My Spirit in the north country."*
>
> Zechariah 6:1-8

Notice that in verse one the four chariots were coming from between two mountains of bronze. Scholars identify these mountains as Mount Zion and the Mount of Olives in Jerusalem. It is my view that they had assembled to sign the Peace Treaty of Daniel 9:27. This Peace Treaty immediately precedes the Tribulation. Now let us direct our attention to verse seven.

Much debate has centered around the words of verse seven, namely who are the "strong steeds?" Since the black, white and dappled horses are enumerated in verse six, I believe the "strong steeds" of verse seven are the red ones. **In both Zechariah and Revelation, only the red horses go to the whole earth.**

Furthermore, I agree with David Baron's translation of verse eight to be correct, as we note that "ruach", translated in King James as "Spirit" can also be translated "anger". Thus the eighth verse should read instead as: *"See, those who go to the north country have caused my anger to rest on the north country".* (Zechariah 6:8) **"The meaning of the 8th verse, then, is that the company of invisible host whose mission was toward the north country caused God's anger to rest on it".**[6] Therefore, when we compare the chariots of Zechariah 6 with the mission of the horsemen in Revelation 6, we will see the events which have caused God's anger to rest on the north country.

THE FOUR HORSEMEN OF THE APOCALYPSE

And so, as I have just indicated, I believe the four horses of Revelation 6 are indeed another look at the four chariots of Zechariah 6. I hold this view for several reasons:

1. The horses of Zechariah's chariots are: red, black, white and dappled (i.e. spotted).

2. The horses of the Apocalypse are: red, black, white and green (pale in KJV). [The mystery of why the "dappled" horses, which I identify as Rome, are

classified as green in the New Testament will be discussed in the next chapter.]

3. Chronologically, the four chariots of Zechariah 6 come on the scene immediately before the coming of Messiah.

4. Likewise, the four horsemen come on the scene at the beginning of the Tribulation seven years before Jesus returns.

[1] *Now I saw when the Lamb opened one of the seals; and I heard one of the four living creatures saying with a voice like thunder, "Come and see."* [2] *And I looked, and behold, a white horse. He **who sat on it had a bow;** and a crown was given to him, and he went out conquering and to conquer.*

[3] *When He opened the second seal, I heard the second living creature saying, "Come and see."* [4] *Another horse, fiery red, went out. And **it was granted to the one who sat on it to take peace from the earth,** and that people should kill one another; and there was given to him a great sword.*

[5] *When He opened the third seal, I heard the third living creature say, "Come and see." So I looked, and behold, a black horse, and **he who sat on it had a pair of scales in his hand.*** [6] *And I heard a voice in the midst of the four living creatures saying, "A quart of wheat for a denarius, and three quarts of barley for a denarius; and do not harm the oil and the wine."*

[7] *When He opened the fourth seal, I heard the voice of the fourth living creature saying, "Come and see."* [8] *So I looked, and behold, a pale horse. And **the name of him who sat on it was Death,** and Hades*

followed with him. And power was given to them over a fourth of the earth, to kill with sword, with hunger, with death, and by the beasts of the earth.
Revelation 6:1-8 (emphasis added)

It is my opinion that the Revived Roman Empire will approximate the borders of the Ancient Roman Empire and the judgments of the first half of the Tribulation are directed primarily toward them.

A combination of the European Union, the Arab states and Israel are called the "Union for the Mediterranean".

The Union for the Mediterranean is a multilateral partnership that encompasses 43 countries from Europe and the Mediterranean Basin: the 27 member states of the European Union and the 16 Mediterranean partner countries from North Africa, the Middle East and the Balkans. It was created in July 2008 during the term of French President Nicholas Sarkozy as a relaunched Euro-Mediterranean Partnership (the Barcelona Process).[7]

It is my view that Germany will not be a member of this coalition during the Tribulation. Germany was not a part of the Ancient Roman Empire. If the endtime coalition is truly the Revived Roman Empire, then it will not include Germany.

Thus, we see a picture of judgment going throughout the Union for the Mediterranean during the first half of the Tribulation. We are calling that the time of The Wrath of the Lamb (Revelation 6:16). A careful reading of the Book of Revelation indicates that there are two different three and a half year periods during the Tribulation. The first half is called the "Wrath of the Lamb", Revelation 6:16, and the second half, the "Wrath of God", Revelation 14:7. For our purpose in this chapter, it is important to see that the assignment of the four horsemen is to bring judgment to the part of earth that surrounds the Mediterranean Sea: Europe, the Middle East, Northern Africa, and also to Russia.

Matching the four chariots of Zechariah with the four horsemen of Revelation, including the direction and purpose of their mission, works together "hand in glove". Zechariah tells us who they are and where they are going. Revelation tells us why.

So, who are they? Again, we trust David Baron to explain:

> *The number four clearly brings to our mind again the four great Gentile world-powers whose successive course makes up "the times of the Gentiles", and whose final overthrow must precede the restoration and blessing of Israel, and the visible establishment of the Messianic Kingdom.*[8]

> *These four are the Babylonia, the Medo-Persian, the Grecian (or Graeco-Macedonian), and the Roman. "These are the horns (or Gentile powers) which have scattered Judah, Israel, and Jerusalem" (chap. (.19), and it is the overthrow and judgment of these, by means of invisible heavenly powers appointed of God as a necessary precursor to the establishment of Messiah's kingdom, and the blessing of Israel, which is symbolically set forth to the prophet in this last vision.*[9]

And so, the mystery is revealed. The first time the chariots are introduced is in Zechariah 6:2-3. They are in chronological order here. We take their identity from these verses. Zechariah 6:2-3 – *²With the first chariot were red horses, with the second chariot black horses, [3] with the third chariot white horses, and with the fourth chariot dappled horses—strong steeds.*

CHRONOLOGICAL ORDER	
Red	Babylon (606 - 536 BC)
Black	Persia (536 - 330 BC)
White	Greece (Alexander The Great)
"Strong Steeds"	Rome (to 476 AD)

Then in Zechariah 6:6-7 we see which direction they are going. This helps us greatly when we come to Revelation. For in Revelation 6 we have their missions explained.

The mission of each horseman will be examined more closely in Chapter 7. The conclusions drawn are based on a combination of:

1. What the scriptures say
2. What Bible teachers have taught
3. Current events
4. Our own interpretation

See the chart on next the page for identity, purpose and direction of the four chariots.

Identity and Purpose of the Four Chariots / Horsemen

	Color	Country	Mission	Direction	Order of Appearance (In Revelation)
1st Chariot	Red	Babylon (Iraq)	Take a sword (Islam/War) throughout the earth	To the whole earth	Second
2nd Chariot	Black	Medo-Persia (Iran)	Famine and hunger, especially in Iran, Russia, and all the countries that fought Israel in the Ezekiel war	North	Third
3rd Chariot	White	Greece	The Assyrian/Greek antichrist leaves Israel after the Peace Treaty of Dan. 9:27 and goes north to coalesce his base	North	First
4th Chariot	Dappled /Green	Rome	Given power over 1/4 of the earth. The evil twins, "Death and Hell" covenant with Israel (Isa. 28). They also kill with war, hunger, beasts of the earth and their own evil spiritual power.	South	Fourth

CHAPTER 5

A DAPPLED GREEN HORSE

As I have stated, the four world powers that are subject to judgment, according to Zechariah and Revelation are:

---

1) Babylon (Iraq) .... Red Horse

2) Medo-Persia (Iran) .... Black Horse

3) Greece .... White Horse

4) Rome .... Dappled/Green Horse

These are the ancient enemies and oppressors of God's chosen people.

In the Book of Daniel these same four empires are first illustrated prophetically in chapter 2, in Nebuchadnezzar's image.

1. Babylon	Head of Gold	Daniel 2:32
2. Medo-Persia	Chest and arms of silver	Daniel 2:32
3. Greece	Belly and thighs of bronze	Daniel 2:32
4. Rome	Legs of iron	Daniel 2:33
5. Revived Rome	Feet of iron and clay	Daniel 2:41-43

Of the feet of iron and clay Daniel says:

> [41] *Whereas you saw the feet and toes, partly of potter's **clay and partly of iron**, the kingdom shall be divided; yet the strength of the iron shall be in it, just as you saw the iron mixed with ceramic clay. [42] And as the toes of the feet were partly of iron and **partly of clay**, so the kingdom shall be partly strong and partly fragile. [43] As you saw **iron mixed with ceramic clay**, they will mingle with the seed of men; but they will not*

*adhere to one another, just as iron does not mix
with clay.*

Daniel 2:41-43 (emphasis added)

Daniel repeats three times the vision of iron mixed with clay. It is possible the feet of the image had a spotted or "dappled" appearance. More than a hundred years later, when Zechariah wrote his book and called the horses of the fourth chariot "dappled", there must have been much curiosity about who this fourth and final kingdom would be Clearly, from the prophets, the Jews could conclude it would be a strong and cruel empire.

DESPISED AND PAGAN ROME

By the time John wrote the book of Revelation on the island of Patmos, all Jews knew who the fourth kingdom was, because they were much oppressed by it. This fourth kingdom was Rome.

John personally had much to fear from Rome. They had tried to boil him in oil, but he didn't die. So Emperor Domitian had him exiled to the island of Patmos.

Let us consider again, the four chariots of Zechariah versus the four horses of the apocalypse. Refer to the chart below.

Kingdom	Zechariah's Chariots	John's Horses
Babylon	Red	Red
Medo-Persia	Black	Black
Greece	White	White
Rome	Dappled	Green

Why does the color not match in the Roman horse? I believe that John knew, as did all the Jewish Christians of his era, that Zechariah and Daniel had prophesied severe judgment would befall the fourth kingdom, according to Scripture. John could not risk his own life and the lives of fellow believers by linking Rome with the books of Zechariah and Daniel. Therefore, I believe, either John or the Lord encoded Rome in a color that would not fit the pattern: chloros, in Greek, or green. (The King James incorrectly identifies the horse as pale. However, the word chloros is used to describe "green grass" in Revelation 8:7 and "neither any green thing" in Revelation 9:4. We get our word "chlorophyll" from this word.)

We observe that John also employed this same vehicle, encoding the name for Rome in Revelation 17. We identify Rome in Revelation 17:9 as a city that sits on seven hills. Also, in Revelation 17:18 Rome is identified as "the great city that reigns over the kings of the earth". The "ten toes" of Daniel 2 are the kings who reign in the revived Roman Empire. A careful reading of Revelation 17 reveals that John calls that city, which is actually Rome, "Mystery Babylon the Great" in verse five, and "the harlot" in verses 15 and 16. Again, I feel this was encoded to prevent the ire of the Romans from falling on the Jewish Christians (See Chapter 11).

The color of the Roman horse, green, will still have significance, of course. Never, in the entire Bible, is a word ever wasted or without meaning. Could it be that the green represents a radical left wing movement that is currently sweeping Europe? I am referring to the environmental movement, which hold that "Mother Earth" is sacred, the Green Movement.

Let us listen to what John says about the fourth (revived Roman Empire) horseman.

*⁸ So I looked, and behold, a pale horse. And the
name of him who sat on it was Death, and Hades
followed with him. And power was given to them
over a fourth of the earth, to kill with sword,
with hunger, with death, and by the beasts of the
earth.*

Revelation 6:8

In my view "killing with hunger" may be related to
forbidding citizens from eating meat, depriving them of an
important source of protein.

Listen to Paul prophesy about abstaining from meat in
the "latter times".

*³ Forbidding to marry, and commanding to <u>abstain
from meats</u>, which God hath created to be received
with thanksgiving of them which believe and
know the truth.*

1 Timothy 4:3-4 KJV

There is presently a movement afoot in Europe,
spearheaded by Beatle Paul McCartney, to force a "meatless
Monday" on the population. Will that evolve into a meatless
society, as animals gain more "rights"?

Going back to Revelation 6:8 we see that people will
also be killed "by the beasts of the earth". Again, this
is a phenomenon we are already seeing, as hunters are
not allowed to thin out the population of bears, deer, and
other wild game animals, in certain areas. (We will discuss
"Death and Hell" further in Chapter 7).

But first, we must consider the War of Ezekiel 38 and
39 in the next chapter of this book. It is my fervent hope
that this war precedes the Tribulation, and I believe it will.
A mighty, worldwide harvest follows this war and I want to
be a participant! The Islamic tradition is to serve a God

of power.   Many Muslims will come to the Lord after the Ezekiel war when they see that Jehovah is, in fact, stronger than Allah!

CHAPTER 6

WORLD CONFLICT/
WORLD HARVEST

When General Titus, the Roman warrior, surrounded and sacked Jerusalem in 70 A.D., the Jews were enslaved and taken to the four corners of the earth. It is a testament to God's faithfulness that they were never assimilated into the culture of any nation to which they were assigned. God had called the Jews to be a holy nation:

> [5] *Now therefore, if you will indeed obey My voice and keep My covenant, then you shall be a special treasure to Me above all people; for all the earth is Mine.* [6] *And you shall be to Me a kingdom of priests and a holy nation.' These are the words*

which you shall speak to the children of Israel."
Exodus 19:5-6

The Jews were required to depart from the promised land three times:

1. During the famine in Jacob's day when they went to Egypt, where they were fed by their brother Joseph, who God had sent ahead to preserve them.
2. In 586 B.C. when King Nebuchadnezzar took them to Babylon for 70 years.
3. In 70 A.D. when Titus the Roman dispersed them throughout the world.

God had always promised them that their ultimate end would be to return to Israel, the center of the earth, to rule and reign with Him forever.

> [14] *Also the sons of those who afflicted you*
> *Shall come bowing to you,*
> *And all those who despised you shall fall prostrate*
> *at the soles of your feet;*
> ***And they shall call you The City of the Lord,***
> ***Zion of the Holy One of Israel.***
> [15] *"Whereas you have been forsaken and hated, So that no one went through you, I will make you an eternal excellence, A joy of many generations.*
> Isaiah 60:14-15 (emphasis added)

> [2] *And behold, the glory of the God of Israel came from the way of the east. His voice was like the sound of many waters; and the earth shone with His glory.*

> [5] *The Spirit lifted me up and brought me into the inner court; and behold, the glory of the Lord filled the temple.*

*⁶ Then I heard Him speaking to me from the temple, while a man stood beside me. ⁷ And He said to me, "Son of man, this is the place of My throne and the place of the soles of My feet, **where I will dwell in the midst of the children of Israel forever.** No more shall the house of Israel defile My holy name, they nor their kings, by their harlotry or with the carcasses of their kings on their high places.*

Ezekiel 43:2, 5-7 (emphasis added)

The nation of Israel was reborn on May 14, 1948. When the United Nations agreed to give the Jews their land back because they had suffered so in the holocaust, literal hell broke loose. Because Jesus Himself will rule and reign from Jerusalem, the devil has refused to allow the Jews to live in peace.

The wars the Jews have endured in modern times include:

1. 1948 – the war for independence
2. The 1956 War
3. 1967 – the Six Day War
4. 1973 – the Yom Kippur War
5. 2000 – the Intifada
6. 2006 – Lebanon War
7. December 2008 – Operation Cast Lead
8. November 2012 – Operation Pillar of Cloud

The final two wars listed were in response to continual rocket attacks from Hamas who controls the Gaza Strip. Muslim warriors willingly give their lives and their families lives to kill Jews. Only God knows how many young Muslims have descended into hell for eternity, awakened to the stark reality that it was not God who encouraged them to commit murder.

The Bible clearly teaches that the devil will once again try to wrest the Holy Land from the grasp of the chosen people. Even now a war called the war of Gog and Magog, or the war of Ezekiel 38 and 39, is on the radar screen, as we look at current events.

Every country has been assigned a special angel to protect it by God. Likewise, Satan has assigned to each country a "chief prince", to destroy it. The chief prince over Russia is a sinister being named "Gog". While no unanimity exists among Bible scholars as to who Gomer and Togarmah are, in general, the players in the Ezekiel War line up as the following:

Biblical Name	Modern Name
Rosh	... Russia
Meshech	... Moscow (Western capital of Russia)
Tubal	... Tobulsk (Eastern capital of Russia)
Persia	... Iran
Ethiopia	... Ethiopia
Libya	... Libya
Gomer	... Germany or Eastern European Islamic Nations
Togarmah	... Turkey
Gog	... The evil spirit ruling Russia

GOD ORDAINS THE ATTACK

The hordes of Gog listed above will come against the tiny country of Israel to plunder and destroy it. What are the events that will precipitate this massive war? As stated in Chapter 3, I believe Syria will invade Israel. Israel will counterattack, leveling Damascus. In the natural it will be the Israeli destruction of Damascus that causes Russia and her allies to invade Israel. An added dimension in Russia's desire to control Israel is the discovery of oil and natural gas off the coast of Haifa in the Mediterranean Sea. It was discovered in 2010, and has the potential to make Israel one of the greatest energy exporting nations in the Middle East. The Israelis named it the "Leviathan" gas field, after the Biblical sea monster. It is more incentive for Russia to attack Israel. However, in the spiritual realm it is God who ordains the attack.

Notice in the following verses depicting the Ezekiel War, where the Lord God Himself is speaking, commanding the nations to invade Israel:

> [7] *"Prepare yourself and be ready, you **and all your companies** that are gathered about you; and be a guard for them. [8] After many days you will be visited. In the latter years **you will come into the land** of those brought back from the sword and gathered from many people on the mountains of Israel, which had long been desolate; they were brought out of the nations, and now all of them dwell safely. [9] **You will ascend**, coming like a storm, covering the land like a cloud, **you and all your troops** and many peoples with you".*
>
> [10] *'**Thus says the Lord God**: "On that day it shall come to pass that thoughts will arise in your mind, and **you will make an evil plan**: [11] You will say, 'I will go up against a land of unwalled villages; I will go to a peaceful people, who dwell safely, all of them dwelling without walls, and having neither bars nor gates'— [12] to take plunder and to take booty, **to stretch out your hand** against the waste places that are again inhabited, and against a people gathered from the nations,*

*who have acquired livestock and goods, who dwell
in the midst of the land.*
Ezekiel 38:7-12 (emphasis added)

The purpose of the war, from the adversary's point of view, is to take plunder and take booty, and to come against Israel, according to verse 12.

The nations of the world, including the United States, will lodge a diplomatic protest, but not interfere militarily.

*[13] Sheba, Dedan, the merchants of Tarshish, and
all their young lions will say to you, 'Have
you come to take plunder? Have you gathered your
army to take booty, to carry away silver and gold,
to take away livestock and goods, to take great
plunder?'"*
Ezekiel 38:13 (emphasis added)

THE JEWS WILL WIN THE WAR

Many Christian scholars consider Americans to be the "young lions of Tarshish". Tarshish is seen by various authors to be the northern Mediterranean area, Spain or England. Since the pilgrims were of European descent, any of the above definitions of the Tarshish would qualify Americans to be their offspring or young lions. Using this same logic, Canadians and Australians may also be defined as "young lions of Tarshish".

Against all odds, the Jews will win the war. To be more precise, the great God, Jehovah, will win the war. He has many weapons at His disposal. They include:

1. Earthquake: Surely in that day there shall be a great earthquake in the land of Israel. Ezekiel 38:20

2. Military Might: *"I will call for a sword against Gog in all My mountains..."* Ezekiel 38:21

3. Friendly Fire: *"...Every man's sword will be against his brother".* Ezekiel 38:21

4. Pestilence and Bloodshed: *"And I will bring him to judgment with pestilence and bloodshed..".* Ezekiel 38:22

5. Rain, Hail, Fire and Brimstone: *"I will rain down on him, on his troops, and on the many peoples who are with him, flooding rain, great hailstones, fire and brimstone".* Ezekiel 38:22

It is my view that the war of Ezekiel 38 and 39 will precede the Tribulation Period. The Church will have her finest hour as God uses us to bring in the great harvest for which we have prepared so long.

Thus, I will present the evidence which I feel places the Ezekiel War before the Tribulation Period. Please see the chart on the following page.

As I have previously indicated, God, who is love, ordered the invasion. But, we might ask, why would He do that?

EVENT	EZEKIEL WAR	ARMAGEDDON Area where the armies assemble Rev. 16:16
Where it will be fought	Mountains of Israel Ezek. 38:21; 39:2	Jerusalem Zech. 12:2; 14:2 Joel 2:32
When it will be fought	6th Day, "Latter Days" Ezek. 38:8; 16	7th Day, Day of the Lord Zech. 14:1; Joel 2:1 Obadiah verse 15 Rev. 1:10
Concluded by	Treaty of Daniel 9:27	Jesus defeating the Nations Zech. 14:3 Rev. 19:11-21
Nations Participating	Russia, Iran, Ethiopia, Libya, Gomer, Turkey Ezek. 38:11	All Goat Nations Zech. 12:3; Zech. 14:3 Rev. 19:11-21
Position of Jerusalem when the war begins	At peace Ezek. 38:11	"Trampled Down" Luke 21:24
Position of Israelis when the war begins	At peace Ezek. 38:14	Hiding in Petra (Messianic Jews) Rev. 12:13-16
Purpose of the war	Bring in the harvest Ezek. 38:16, 23 Ezek. 39:7, 21	Set up the millennial reign with Israel presiding Isa. 42:4; Zech. 14:16-21 Rev. 20:4

1. God is just and must bring judgment on those who come against His chosen People.

[19] For in My jealousy and in the fire of My wrath I have spoken..".

Ezekiel 38:19

2. God is merciful and this war will trigger the great world harvest.

*[16] "...**so that the nations may know Me,** when I am hallowed in you, O God, before their eyes".*

Ezekiel 38:16 (emphasis added)

*[23] "Thus I will magnify Myself and sanctify Myself, and **I will be known in the eyes of many nations.** Then they shall know that I am the Lord".*

Ezekiel 38:23 (emphasis added)

*[7] "So I will make My holy name known in the midst of My people Israel, and I will not let them profane my name anymore. Then **the nations shall know that I am the Lord**, the Holy One in Israel.*

Ezekiel 39:7 (emphasis added)

*[21] "I will set My glory among the nations; **all the nations shall see My judgment** which I have executed, and My hand which I have laid on them".*

Ezekiel 39:21 (emphasis added)

3. Israel will finally, as a nation, turn back to Jehovah (however, they will not recognize their Messiah yet).

*[22] "So the house of Israel shall know that **I am the***

Lord *their God from that day forward"*.

Ezekiel 39:22 (emphasis added)

Let us pause here to reflect on the lifestyle of the modern man and woman. Most of us watch television for two to four hours a day. Since the Vietnam conflict, we have become accustomed to watching war on television.

In the Iraqi War in 2003, we even had reporters "embedded" with the troops, so we could watch the war unfold, "play by play". How many hours a day did we watch television during the war? Thus it has become a part of our national psyche to see war "live and in color" on our television set.

A MUSLIM/RUSSIAN ALLIANCE FORMED TO TEACH ISRAEL A LESSON

Use your own imagination and project yourself into the days of the Ezekiel War. We are alarmed to see Russian troops moving into position! An alliance, much like our coalition against Iraq, will probably coalesce. Nations will decide to "teach Israel a lesson", once and for all. It has to happen, because God spoke it through Ezekiel.

Television newsmen will be bringing us updates, minute by minute. Christians will, no doubt, be holding prayer meetings around the clock: *"Father, let Your will be done on earth as it is in heaven"*. Nominal Christians and fence sitters will dust off the Word and check it out - Ezekiel 38 & 39.

Suddenly, the attack! Paratroopers descend on the mountains of Israel, *"covering the land like a cloud"*, — Ezekiel 38:9 — *"all your troops and many peoples"* against a country of 5,000,000 Jews. (Flashback to Gideon, who defeated innumerable Midianites with 300 men.) Could it really be? Could the Bible be true?

– 78 –

And then, earthquake, sword, fire and brimstone, hail and rain. God reigns, He really is in control. Oh praise Him forevermore!

Nations, yes nations, will come to the Lord. This will be the great harvest for which we have waited so long. We will reap where we have not sown, the plowman will overtake the reaper; and the former and the latter rain together. The knowledge of the glory of the Lord will cover the land as the water covers the seas, and we will be right in the middle of it all.

Christians open their Bibles to Ezekiel 38 and read fast and furiously. Someone knocks at your door, the phone rings, the same question from every neighbor, every friend, "You're a Christian aren't you? What's happening?" Saints of God, learn it now, so you will be prepared. We must respond rightly. We will tell them, "This is only the beginning. God is judging the nations. Repent, and be saved. Accept Jesus and escape the wrath to come".

> [34] *"But take heed to yourselves, lest your hearts be weighed down with carousing, drunkenness, and cares of this life, and that Day come on you unexpectedly.* [35] *For it will come as a snare on all those who dwell on the face of the whole earth.* [36] *Watch therefore, and pray always* **that you may be counted worthy to escape all these things that will come to pass,** *and to stand before the Son of Man".*

> Luke 21:34-36 (emphasis added)

> [9] ***For God did not appoint us to wrath,*** *but to obtain salvation through our Lord Jesus Christ,* [10] *who died for us that whether we wake or sleep, we should live together with Him.*

> 1 Thessalonians 5:9-10 (emphasis added)

> *10 Because you have kept My command to persevere, I also will keep you from the hour of trial which shall **come upon the whole world, to test those who dwell on the earth.** 11 Behold, I am coming quickly! Hold fast what you have, that no one may take your crown.*
>
> Revelation 3:10-11 (emphasis added)

IT'S TIME TO SET YOUR HEART ON COURSE

Dear Saints of God, we are being called by the Holy Spirit in this hour to prepare. Now is the time to begin, if you have not already heard His command: longer seasons of prayer every day, taking communion, regular seasons of fasting, joining a cell group, studying and meditating in the Word, enrolling in that Bible Study offered by your Church, or using your vacation to attend a good Christian seminar. In short, it's time to set your heart on course so you will be found *"without spot or wrinkle"*.

Some will not accept the mantle, however. Sadly, they will miss the Rapture. It will be their lot to see a Syrian diplomat travel to Israel to negotiate a peace treaty with the victorious and ebullient Israelis. It is my view that his offer will include allowing the Jews to rebuild the temple on Mount Moriah. They have been yearning for a temple since 70 A.D., and it's too good a deal to turn down. Why will a Syrian be the negotiator? Possibly because Syria had lost the most. Their capital, Damascus, had been destroyed. In any event the Bible is clear, he is the Antichrist, coming to the Israelis with a seven-year peace treaty:

> *27 "Then he shall confirm a covenant with many for one week; but in the middle of the week he shall bring an end to sacrifice and offering. And, on the wing of abominations shall be one who makes*

desolate, even until the consummation, which is determined, is poured out on the desolate".

Daniel 9:27

As we review Daniel 7:10 and 11 we notice that the first thing Daniel heard when the books were opened was the sound of the Antichrist's voice.

[10] *...The judgment was set, and the books were opened.*

[11] *I beheld then because of the voice of the great words* ***which the horn spake...***

Daniel 7:10, 11 (KJV emphasis added)

Why was the Antichrist's voice the first thing Daniel heard when Jesus opened the seals? The first four seals in Revelation 6 release the four horsemen of the Apocalypse. Does the first seal release the Antichrist?

Read on to see if the Book of Revelation agrees with what we have just read here in the Book of Daniel.

CHAPTER 7

THE FOUR HORSEMEN EXPLAINED

PART 1 - THE RIDER ON THE WHITE HORSE

3rd Chariot	On the White Horse	Represents Greece	The Antichrist leaves Israel after the Peace Treaty of Dan. 9:27 and goes North to coalesce his base	Goes North	First to appear in Revelation

¹ Now I saw when the Lamb opened one of the seals; and I heard one of the four living creatures say with a voice like thunder, "Come and see". ² And

> *! behold, a white horse. He who sat*
> *nw; and a crown was given to him,*
> *ut conquering and to conquer.*
>
> Revelation 6:1-2

...naos and confusion, due to the millions (perhaps billions) of saints who have disappeared in the Rapture. But sadly, in the 21st century, America's preeminence began to wane. Overspending, rejection of the Judeo-Christian culture and the increased influence of socialist principles took their toll. America had been the conscience of the world. As peace-keeper, chastiser of rogue nations and provider of food, aid and medicine to the poor, she has had no equal. However, in the revival that accompanies the Ezekiel War, most Americans will recommit their lives to the Lord Jesus. Therefore it is possible that 100 million Americans depart in the Rapture. (This is our fervent prayer.)

The world needs leadership. They turn for help to the brilliant diplomat who did what no one else could do - brought peace to the Middle East. This man, Antichrist, is given a bow, military power, and a crown, legal authority, to assume power in the Muslim World. Going north from Jerusalem, he unites the following Muslim nations which are in chaos for the reasons listed:

Syria – devastated by the leveling of Damascus.

Iraq – now a client state of Iran.

Iran and Turkey – These countries (as well as Russia, Libya and Ethiopia) have lost 84% of their young men in the Ezekiel War. Never in modern warfare has there been such devastation.

> [1] *...Behold, I am against thee, Oh Gog, the prince of Meshech and Tubal,*

300 million ped

[2] And I will turn thee back, and leave but a sixth part of thee,...

Ezekiel 39:1-2 KJV (emphasis added)

The fact that a "sixth part" will be left implies 84% will die.

Lebanon – under the influence of Iran and Syria, they join the coalition for security reasons.

Therefore, we see the Antichrist, an Islamic military leader, going north from Israel to create an alliance of these countries: Lebanon, Syria, Iran, Iraq and Turkey. In ancient times these countries had often been one big confederation known as the "Fertile Crescent". All pagan religions found their genesis in the Fertile Crescent where many deities were worshipped. Abraham was called out of Iraq in the Fertile Crescent to separate himself unto God.

I believe that the Antichrist will rule out of the Fertile Crescent for the first three and a half years of the Tribulation Period. He will probably spend much time at the headquarters of the European Union which is presently in Brussels, Belgium.

He will also have a "home base" from which to operate. In ancient times the leading cities of the Fertile Crescent were Ninevah and Babylon. Babylon will be the center of economic power during the second half of the Tribulation Period according to Zechariah 5:5-11 and Revelation 18. Expect Brussels, Belgium to be the economic center of the World during the first half of the Tribulation and Babylon during the second half. It is worthy to note that kings of Assyria, Babylon, Persia and Greece all had palaces in the ancient city of Babylon. Alexander the Great who conquered the known world died in Babylon. The Bible clearly relates the Antichrist to these four countries. He is referred to in Scripture as:

[handwritten: "Sheep" = Followers of Christ]

[handwritten: The "Goat" = No believers]

1. The Assyrian – Micah 5:5-6
2. The King of Babylon – Isaiah 14:4
3. He has feet like a bear (Persian implied) – Revelation 13:2
4. Son of Greece – Zechariah 9:13

The following chart describes how Antichrist defeats the Sunni during the first half of the Tribulation.

	ANTICHRIST'S EXPEDITIONS	
1.	Daniel 11:40	Attacked by Egypt, Antichrist musters 200 million man army (Revelation 9)
2.	Daniel 11:41	Invades Israel; Ignores Jordan
3.	Daniel 11:42, 43	Attacks Egypt again, also Libya and Ethiopia
4.	Revelation 17	Orders Rome destroyed
5.	Daniel 11:44	Attacks east (China?) and north (Russia?)
6.	Daniel 11:45; 12:11	Establishes palace in Israel (mid Tribulation) Sets up Abomination of Desolation

How do we know that Daniel 11:40-45 refers to the first half of the Tribulation?

1. In verse 45 he resides in Jerusalem. This parallels Revelation 11:7-10. Notice that John changes the

name of Jerusalem to "Sodom and Egypt" as soon as Antichrist takes over (Revelation 11:8).

2. Daniel 12:1 is a parallel verse to Revelation 12:7, another mid Tribulation event. Thus, Daniel 11:40-45 occur during the first half of the Tribulation. Here we see Antichrist conquer the Roman Empire in the Book of Daniel.

Therefore I conclude that the rider on the white horse, the Antichrist, conquers the Muslim world first, and sets up his headquarters in Babylon/and Brussels. For those who have been erroneously taught that the rider on the white horse is Jesus, I would point this out. Jesus cannot be on the white horse since He is in heaven breaking the seven seals (Revelation 6:1).

PART II - THE RIDER ON THE RED HORSE

Before we embark on an explanation of the rider on the red horse, it is important to understand the history of monotheistic religion. Monotheistic religion is the belief in only one God. There are only three major monotheistic religions: Judaism, Christianity and Islam. All three hold Abraham to be their father.

All three of these religions believe a ruler will rise up from their religion at the end of days to rule the world. Amazingly, all three are correct, setting up the climax of human history!

Jewish doctrine states:
I believe with complete faith that Messiah will come, and though he tarries I will wait for him every coming day.

Christian doctrine states:
God will send Jesus, whom heaven must receive until the time of the restoration of all things (Acts 3:21).

Muslim doctrine states:

Fight until all declare there is no God but Allah and Mohammad is his prophet.

Furthermore, the Muslims are waiting for an Islamic prophet to come out of the desert at the end of days to lead the entire world into the Islamic faith.

Islam leaves no room for compromise. It is their avowed purpose to win the world. A recent Al Qaida memorandum,run on an Islamic web site adjures Muslims to "**...return to the path, to separate themselves from non-believers, to become their enemies and to fight holy war against them by money, word and weapons. This enemy must be fought, there is no other way but to...eradicate it".**[10]

It is my opinion that Jews, Christians, and Muslims will all see their heroes on the center stage of world history very soon. First, the Antichrist will appear as the rider on the white horse. He will be a Muslim political leader. Seven years later the Jews will see Messiah, as He sets His feet on the Mount of Olives. No surprise to those who accepted Jesus after the Rapture. The Jewish Messiah is none other than our own Lord and Savior, Jesus Christ.

Let us now consider the rider on the red horse:

1st Chariot	On the Red Horse	Represents Babylon (Iraq)	Takes a sword (Islam) throughout the earth	Goes to the whole Earth	Second to appear in Revelation

Now happening?

[3] When He opened the second seal, I heard the second living creature saying, "Come and see." [4] Another horse, fiery red, went out. And it was granted to

To Come?

the one who sat on it to take peace from the earth,
and that people should kill one another; and there
was given to him a great sword

Revelation 6:3-4

It is interesting to note that the rider on the red horse is the only horseman given permission to go throughout the whole earth. In fact, in Zechariah 6:7 we are told three times that the red chariot goes to the whole earth.

7 Then the strong steeds went out, eager to go, that
they might walk to and fro throughout the earth.
And He said, "Go, walk to and fro throughout the
earth". So they walked to and fro throughout the
earth.

Approximately 1.5 billion of the 6.75 billion people living today are Muslim. Mosques are springing up in traditionally Christian countries at an alarmingly rapid rate.

Martyrdom of infidels – those who do not accept Allah, and Mohammad as his prophet – has historically been an acceptable way to spread Islam. Thus, we are not surprised to see that the rider on the red horse is given a "great sword". I believe the "great sword" represents Islam and the Muslim fundamentalists who spread their faith by the sword. Decapitation has long been a method of execution in Eastern cultures. The Philistines beheaded King Saul (I Samuel 31:9) and Herod had John the Baptist beheaded (Matthew 14:8). In recent history, Daniel Pearl, a Jewish New York Times reporter, was beheaded by the Pakistanis in 2002. Since 2002, thousands of people have been beheaded by Islamic extremists. Therefore, we should not be surprised to learn that martyrdom by decapitation will be used against followers of Jesus during the Tribulation Period:

4 And I saw thrones, and they sat on them, and

judgment was committed to them. Then I saw the **souls of those who had been beheaded** *for their witness to Jesus and for the word of God, who had not worshiped the beast or his image, and had not received his mark on their foreheads or on their hands. And they lived and reigned with Christ for a thousand years.*

Revelation 20:4 (emphasis added)

The world had expected the Antichrist to usher in an era of peace and security. He was the architect of the brilliant peace plan after the Ezekiel War. What were the terms of this Peace Treaty that I believe is signed after the Rapture? Let me give my opinion.

(POSSIBLE) TERMS OF PEACE TREATY OF DANIEL 9:27

1. There will be a Jewish state under Israeli control, a Palestinian state under Arab control.

2. The Old City of Jerusalem will be without sovereignty, with peace administered by an international body.

3. Palestinian refugees will have the "right of return" to Palestinian areas only, which are demilitarized.

4. Israel will have the Western Wall, but revert back to the pre-1967 borders with land swaps.

5. The Jews will rebuild the Temple next to the Dome of the Rock after Elijah returns and allows it. (Mark 9:12)

> [1b] *"Rise and measure the temple of God, the altar, and those who worship there. [2] But* ***leave out the court which is outside the temple, and do not measure it, for it has been***

given to the Gentiles. And they will tread the holy city underfoot for forty-two months".
Revelation 11:1b, 2 (emphasis added)

In previous generations it was believed that the Jews would never build the Temple next to an idolatrous Islamic edifice. However, today many believe that when Elijah returns, he will give the Jews permission to do exactly that. Notice in the above passage from Revelation 11, there is clearly a "gentile court" next to the Temple.

However, the Antichrist also gives his Islamic followers permission to go throughout the world, spreading the Muslim ideology by the sword. Therefore, there will be no peace. The great apostle Paul had forewarned them:

> [2] *For you yourselves know perfectly that the day of the Lord so comes as a thief in the night.*
> [3] *For when they say,* **"Peace and safety!"** *then* **sudden destruction comes upon them,** *as labor pains upon a pregnant woman. And they shall not escape.*
> I Thessalonians 5:2-3 (emphasis added)

The rider on the white horse, the Antichrist, goes north. The rider on the red horse goes to the whole world. Next, we will consider the rider on the black horse who also travels north.

2nd Chariot	On the Black Horse	Represents Medo-Persia (Iran)	Famine and hunger in Iran, Russia and all the countries that fought Israel in the Ezekiel war	Goes North	Third to appear in Revelation

PART III - THE RIDER ON THE BLACK HORSE

We see in Zechariah 6:6 that the rider on the black horse actually precedes the Antichrist (the rider on the white horse) into the north country.

> *6 The one with the black horses is going to the north country, the white are going after them, and the dappled are going toward the south country.*
>
> Zechariah 6:6

The black horses represent famine and ride to the north country, Iran and possibly Russia.

THE BONDING TOGETHER OF ISLAM AND COMMUNISM

Let us consider the rider on the black horse according to the translation of Zechariah 6:8 provided for us by David Baron in the book <u>Zechariah: A Commentary On His Visions And Prophecy</u>.

> *8 See those who go to the north country have caused my anger to rest on the north country.[11]*

In the spirit realm the Ezekiel War had been precipitated by the bonding together of two very powerful and very evil spirits: Islam and Communism. God's anger had rested on the countries whose leaders embraced these spirits. Thus, these countries had reaped judgment: Iran, Turkey, and Russia. All of the above—the north country—have been bastions of anti-Semitism for generations. They have persecuted God's chosen people, the apple of His eye. Beginning during the Ezekiel War and progressing through the Tribulation Period, they will be reaping all the evil they have sown.

John sees that the rider on the black horse who was sent to the north country has a pair of scales in his hand. During the episode with the four horsemen the only direct quotation John hears is spoken when the black horse is released. John hears a voice speaking from heaven. Let us consider what the voice says:

> *⁶ And I heard a voice in the midst of the four living creatures saying, "A quart of wheat for a denarius; and three quarts of barley for a denarius: and do not harm the oil and the wine".*
>
> Revelation 6:6

In John's day a denarius was one day's wages for a laborer. This quote seems to imply that an entire day's pay will be needed to buy mere staple foods to subsist on. In fact, this kind of severe poverty already exists in some third world countries.

Some Biblical scholars believe the words "and do not harm the oil and wine" indicate that a few, probably the leadership of these countries, will live in excessive luxury while their people suffer. We saw a clear picture of that scenario in Saddam Hussein's Iraq. What is the cause of the famine in Iran? First of all, the sanctions applied by the West, because of their nuclear ambitions, have severely stressed their economy. Secondly, they will lose 5/6 of their military men in the Ezekiel War.

Thus, we have a dismal scene in the countries north of Israel. Scarcity of food, starvation which causes disease to flourish, inconsolable grief at the loss of so much life, and a shortage of manpower due to the deaths of the military. Conditions are ripe for this Hitler-like anti-hero, who rides to the north country. The people will no doubt be eager to hear his diabolical plan to make them powerful and wealthy again!

Now let's examine the final horse and its riders.

4th Chariot	On the Green Horse	Represents Rome	Given power over 1/4 of the earth. The evil twins, "Death and Hell," kill with war, hunger, beasts of the earth and their own evil spiritual power.	Goes South	Fourth to appear in Revelation

PART IV - THE RIDERS ON THE GREEN HORSE

Before we discuss the riders associated with the fourth and final horse, we must clarify who they are. Their names are Death and Hell, and they appear together throughout the Bible.

To understand Death and Hell, we must first comprehend this truth:

In the Bible the same name is often given to people and to a geographic location.

Thus, we will see that Death and Hell are evil spirits, and also a place where spirits go.

We will look at several examples. To help solidify this concept in our thinking refer to the chart on the following page.

NAME	REPRESENTS PEOPLE/SPIRITS	REPRESENTS GEOGRAPHICAL LOCATION
Jerusalem	Matt. 23-37 "O Jerusalem, Jerusalem...I wanted to gather your children together."	John 5:1 "Jesus went up to Jerusalem,"
Israel	Matt.2:6 "...Who will shepherd My people Israel?"	Matt. 2:20 "...go into the land of Israel"
Bride of Christ	Rev. 19:7 "...the marriage of the Lamb has come and His wife has made herself ready."	Rev. 21:9, 10 "Come, I will show you the bride, the Lamb's wife... and (he) showed me the great city."
Death and Hell	Rev. 6:8 "...the name of him who sat on it was Death and Hades followed with him."	Rev. 20:13 "...Death and Hades delivered up the dead who were in them."

Death and Hell are seen working together throughout the Bible. Their purpose is always to destroy men's souls.

Let us consider now some of the nefarious deeds of Death and Hell:

1. They incited the demented King Saul to try to destroy David.

6 The sorrows of Sheol surround me; the snares of death confronted me.

II Samuel 22:6

2. The apostle Paul quotes the final victory over them in I Corinthians 15:55:

55 O Death, where is your sting?
O Hades, where is your victory?"

3. Jesus Himself refers to them as a place:

> [18] *"I am He who lives, and was dead, and behold, I am alive forevermore, Amen. And I have the keys of Hades and of Death.*
>
> Revelation 1:18

4. It is "death and hell" (the spirits controlling the Revived Roman Empire) that the Antichrist represents when he makes the peace treaty with Israel. In fact, twice in Isaiah 28 this peace treaty is called the "Covenant with Death and Hell". God hold the Jews at fault for signing this covenant. He accuses their leaders of being "drunk", figuratively speaking. They commit the sin so prominent in Old Testament times. They trust in the "arm of the flesh" (in this case Egypt/Rome) to keep them safe, instead of God. In this passage God is speaking against the Jewish leaders who sign the Peace Treaty of Daniel 9:27.

> [7] *But they also have erred through wine, And through intoxicating drink are out of the way; The priest and the prophet have erred through intoxicating drink, They are swallowed up by wine, They are out of the way through intoxicating drink; They err in vision, they stumble in judgment.*
> [8] ***For all tables are full of vomit and filth;*** *No place is clean.*
> [14] *Therefore hear the word of the Lord, you scornful men, Who rule this people who are in Jerusalem,*
> [15] *Because you have said, **"We have made a covenant with death,***

And with Sheol we are in agreement.
When the overflowing scourge passes through,
It will not come to us,
For we have made lies our refuge,
And under falsehood we have hidden ourselves".
[18] *Your covenant with death will be annulled,*
And your agreement with Sheol will not stand;
When the overflowing scourge passes through,
Then you will be trampled down by it.
Isaiah 28:7, 8; 14, 15; 18 (emphasis added)

It is my guess that the "overflowing scourge" is Iran/or the Antichrist. Israel has trusted the Assyrian Antichrist as an agent of the Revived Roman Empire to guarantee the peace.

In a double cross during the first half of the Tribulation, Antichrist teams up with Iran and attacks Egypt and bombs Rome (see the destruction of Rome in Chapter 11 of this book). In Daniel we see the Antichrist's attack on North Africa, part of the Revived Roman Empire. (It is my view that Antichrist's army referenced in Daniel 11:40 is the 200 million man army of Revelation 9:16).

[40] *"At the time of the end the king of the South (Egypt) shall attack him; (Antichrist) and the king of the North (Antichrist) shall come against him (Egypt) like a whirlwind, with chariots, horsemen, and with many ships; and he shall enter the countries, overwhelm them, and pass through.* [41] *He (Antichrist) shall also enter the Glorious Land, (Israel) and many countries shall be overthrown; but these shall escape from his hand: Edom, Moab, and the prominent people of Ammon (Jordon).* [42] *He shall stretch out his*

hand against the countries, and the land of Egypt shall not escape. ⁴³ He shall have power over the treasures of gold and silver, and over all the precious things of Egypt; also the Libyans and Ethiopians shall follow at his heels. ⁴⁴ But news from the east (China) and the north (Russia) shall trouble him; therefore he shall go out with great fury to destroy and annihilate many. ⁴⁵ And he shall plant the tents of his palace between the seas (Mediterranean and Dead Seas) and the glorious holy mountain; yet he shall come to his end, and no one will help him.

Daniel 11:40-45 (parenthesis added)

As we read Revelation 6:8, we notice that only Death sits on the green horse. Hell, or Hades, follows with him. They are the Revived Roman Empire. We will now investigate their assignment as the judgment of planet earth continues.

⁷ *When He opened the fourth seal, I heard the voice of the fourth living creature saying, "Come and see".*

⁸ *So I looked, and behold, a pale (green) horse. And the name of him who sat on it was Death, and Hades followed with him. And power was given to them over a fourth of the earth, to kill with sword, with hunger, with death, and by the beasts of the earth.*

Revelation 6:7, 8 (parenthesis added)

The ruling cities during the Tribulation are shown in the chart on the next page.

RULING CITIES DURING TRIBULATION		
	First Half of Tribulation	**Second Half of Tribulation**
	Various Kings Rule	**Antichrist w/10 Kings**
	Kings of Revived Roman Empire Revelation 6:7, 8	King of Babylon (Isaiah 14:4; Revelation 13:5)
Religious Center	Rome (Revelation 17: 9, 18)	Jerusalem (Daniel 9:27; Revelation 11:8)
Economic Center	Brussels, Belgium (not in Bible because established later)	Babylon (Zechariah 5:5-11; Revelation 18)

I conclude this chapter with the release of the four horsemen. This begins the seven year era known as the Tribulation Period. The reader is encouraged to continue on, reading what John the beloved apostle was so diligent to record.

We began this chapter with the earth in chaos due to the Rapture of the Church. Dear reader, are you ready for the Rapture? Some will answer like this: "I don't want to be Raptured. I like my life the way it is". But life is not going to continue on as it is.

Once women were told they could have an abortion in the first trimester when there was only "a mass of protoplasm" in their uterus. Today, full term babies' brains are sucked out in the birth canal while they are being delivered.

Once terrorism occurred in strange lands far away among uncivilized people. Today, no one is safe anywhere, not even in America.

Once, a bank robbery made headlines in the local newspapers. Today CEO's of high tech companies bilk their shareholders out of billions of dollars.

Once, prostitution was called a "victimless crime". Today, human trafficking, selling children as sex slaves, goes on in all countries, even America.

Once, what people did in their own bedrooms, behind closed doors was their own business. Today those same people have lewd parades in our major cities, handcuffing and whipping each other as they march along.

Jesus promised that at the end of the age, evil would become so evil that everyone would be able to recognize it.

> *24 Another parable He put forth to them, saying: "The kingdom of heaven is like a man who sowed good seed in his field; 25 but while men slept, his enemy came and sowed tares among the wheat and went his way. 26 But when the grain had sprouted and produced a crop, then the tares also appeared".*
>
> *30 **Let both grow together until the harvest, and at the time of harvest I will say to the reapers, "First gather together the tares and bind them in bundles to burn them, but gather the wheat into my barn".***
>
> *39 The enemy who sowed them is the devil, **the harvest is the end of the age**, and the reapers are the angels.*
>
> Matthew 13:24-26, 30, 39 (emphasis added)

We are now in harvest time, the end of the age. The tares are being bundled, which is why sin is now so frank and bold. **You will not be able to continue in your comfortable life, but you can be part of the glorious Church.**

CHAPTER 8

THE GLORIOUS FUTURE
OF
THE GLORIOUS CHURCH

God sees three groups of people on the earth: the Jews, the nations, and the Church.

[32] Give none offence, neither to the Jews, nor to the Gentiles, nor to the church of God:

1 Corinthians 10:32 (KJV)

Much confusion has entered into our understanding of the Church's role by trying to fit the Church into Old Testament Scriptures. Truly there are layers of meaning in Scriptures, and we may appropriate them for our walk of faith. However, the Old Testament was written to the Jews. The Church is not in the Old Testament. The role of the Jews will be considered in greater detail in Chapter 12. To understand the destiny of the nations, let us consider the words of Jesus Himself. He refers in this passage to events after His return to earth at Armageddon to save the Jews from annihilation:

> [31] *"When the Son of Man comes in His glory, and all the holy angels with Him, then He will sit on the throne of His glory.* [32] *All the nations will be gathered before Him, and He will separate them one from another, as a shepherd divides his sheep from the goats.* [33] *And He will set the sheep on His right hand, but the goats on the left.* [34] *Then the King will say to those on His right hand, 'Come, you blessed of My Father, inherit the kingdom prepared for you from the foundation of the world:*
>
> Matthew 25: 31–34, 41

Thus, Jesus will allow the sheep nations to live on earth during the Millennium. The goat nations will go to hell. The stage is being set for Jesus' return, even as I write this book. Nations are polarizing, for good or for evil. The litmus test, so to speak, is this: Do you love God and His chosen people, the Jews?

Those who will be judged "sheep" nations will love and protect the Jews. The "goat" nations will hate and abuse them. Both King David and his worship leader Asaph were given glimpses of the end of this age. They must have had very dramatic conversations, as they compared notes on what God had revealed to them!

WHAT KING DAVID WROTE:

> [1] *Why do the nations rage,*
>   *And the people plot a vain thing?*

> [2] *The kings of the earth set themselves,*
> *And the rulers take counsel together,*
> *Against the Lord and against His Anointed,*
> *saying,*
> [3] *"Let us break Their bonds in pieces*
> *And cast away Their cords from us."*
>
> Psalm 2:1–3

Today as the kings of the earth (United Nations, Arab Confederation and European Union) set themselves against God and Israel, they are inviting the judgments of God to fall on them.

WHAT ASAPH WROTE:

> [1] *Do not keep silent, O God!*
> *Do not hold Your peace,*
> *And do not be still, O God!*
> [2] *For behold, Your enemies make a tumult;*
> *And those who hate You have lifted up their*
> *head.*
> [3] *They have taken crafty counsel against Your*
> *people,*
> *And consulted together against Your sheltered*
> *ones.*
> [4] *They have said, **"Come, and let us cut them***
> ***off from being a nation,***
> ***That the name of Israel may be remembered***
> ***no more."***
>
> Psalm 83:1–4 (emphasis added)

It is the ultimate end of those who would try to cut off Israel from being a nation to be defeated at Armageddon by Jesus Himself.

Dear reader, if you commit your life to Jesus, you can escape the wrath to come. By accepting Jesus, you can extricate yourself from the group called "the nations", and become a part of the group called "the Church". Jesus' own Word declares the end for those who reject Him: *"...the furnace of fire. There will be wailing and gnashing of teeth"* (Matthew 13:42).

The world's answer rings out loudly, "I don't want to serve any God who sends people to hell". Neither do I. **God does not send people to hell!** People choose hell. God is a Spirit; He made man in His image. As God can have no end, neither can we. You must live on in perpetuity, because spirits can never cease to be.

The Father dwells in a wonderful planet called heaven, with His son Jesus sitting at His right hand. Everyone there has a home (John 14:2), an assignment, and a "life". Much time in heaven is spent in worship services, praising the Father and Jesus. Would you enjoy doing that?

If your answer is a resounding, "No, Never!" then friend, you just chose hell. You see there are only two places for spirits to go when they leave the body.

Hell wasn't created for you; it was created for the devil and his angels (Matthew 25:41). However, it had to be enlarged to accommodate rebellious people (Isaiah 5:14). Ultimately, you must choose for yourself. You will not be able to stand before God and say "Lord, I didn't know". By virtue of the fact that you are reading this book, and by the many other witnesses God has sent into your life—you know! All you will be able to say is, "Lord, I chose not to believe". Dear friend, I earnestly adjure you, do not select that path.

> [19] *...I have set before you life and death, blessing and cursing; therefore choose life, that both you and your descendants may live;* [20] ***that you may love the Lord your God,*** *that you may obey*

His voice, and that you may cling to Him, for He
is your life and the length of your days;..."
Deuteronomy 30:19-20 (emphasis added)

And now, dear reader, prepare to look into the future of the glorious Church. There are three possible roads for you to travel while you still live on planet earth. You may belong to only one group: the Jews, the nations, or the Church (1 Corinthians 10:32).

If you choose to be part of the Church, here is your destiny:

1. Walk into greater joy and power as you grow in love and learn to appropriate what Jesus died to give you (see page 207 of this book).

2. Be Raptured before the Tribulation begins.

3. Enjoy the seven year celebration in heaven, while the earth is being judged.

4. Rule and reign over the entire universe with Jesus forever (Matthew 24:47; Revelation 21:7).

THE RAPTURE OF THE CHURCH

Jesus spoke of the catching away of the Church several times.

[40] *And this is the will of Him who sent Me, that*
everyone who sees the Son and believes in Him
*may have everlasting life; and **I will raise him***
up at the last day.
John 6:40 (emphasis added)

He adjures us to pray, that we might escape the Tribulation.

*Watch therefore, and pray always **that you may be counted worthy to escape** all these things that will come to pass, **and to stand before the Son of Man**.*

Luke 21:36 (emphasis added)

Sometimes, the disciples did not "catch on" to all that Jesus taught them. For example, Jesus clearly directed them to take the gospel to the whole world.

[15] And He said to them, "Go into all the world and preach the gospel to every creature".

Mark 16:15

However, it wasn't until Peter saw the sheet with the unclean animals and went to Cornelius' house in Acts 10:45 that they comprehended this truth.

Likewise, while Jesus had taught on the "catching away" of the Church before the Tribulation, the disciples didn't seem to understand (the popular name for the catching away is the rapture of the Church).

God allowed the great apostle Paul to clearly relate the doctrine of the Rapture of the Church. A timeline of some of the events in Paul's life related to his Rapture teaching can be found in the chart below.

Jesus Crucified	Paul Saved On The Road To Damascus	Paul Wrote 1 & 2 Thessalonians	Paul Wrote 1 Corinthians	Paul Martyred In Rome
32 A.D.	35 A.D.	50 A.D.	56 A.D.	66-67 A.D.

The letters to the Thessalonians were the first epistles ever written. That makes the Rapture doctrine one of Christianity's oldest beliefs!

1. Paul saw Jesus in visions (Acts 22:18; Acts 26:12- 18).
2. Paul visited heaven (2 Corinthians 12:2).
3. Paul learned about Communion directly from Jesus (1 Corinthians 11:23).

We will now study exactly what Paul revealed to the infant Church in the first letter he ever wrote in 50 A.D., regarding the Rapture of the Church.

> *[14] For if we believe that Jesus died and rose again, even so God will bring with Him **those who sleep in Jesus.***
> *[15] For this we say to you by the word of the Lord, that we who are alive and remain until the coming of the Lord **will by no means precede those who are asleep.** [16] For the Lord Himself will descend from heaven with a shout, with the voice of an archangel, and with the trumpet of God. And the dead in Christ will rise first. [17] **Then we who are alive and remain shall be caught up together with them in the clouds to meet the Lord in the air.** And thus we shall always be with the Lord.*
>
> 1 Thessalonians 4:14-17 (emphasis added)

(Paul uses the word "sleep" instead of the offensive word "dead" much as we use the term "passed away" today.)

In the next chapter he warns them that the Day of the Lord (begins with The Great Tribulation) will come as a surprise to the nations.

> [1] *But concerning the times and the seasons, brethren, you have no need that I should write to you.* [2] *For you yourselves know perfectly that the day of the Lord so comes as a thief in the night.* [3] *For when they say, "Peace and safety!" then sudden destruction comes upon them, as labor pains upon a pregnant woman. And they shall not escape.* [4] *But you, brethren, are not in darkness, so that this Day should overtake you as a thief.*
>
> [9] **For God did not appoint us to wrath, but to obtain salvation through our Lord Jesus Christ,** [10] **who died for us, that whether we wake or sleep, we should live together with Him.**
>
> 1 Thessalonians 5:1-4; 9-10 (emphasis added)

In the Scripture above, we have an example of the Sower (God the Father) sowing the seed (the doctrine of the Rapture). According to Mark 4:15, "...Satan comes immediately and takes away the word that was sown in their hearts". That is exactly what happened in Thessalonica! Satan immediately sent false teachers to the Thessalonian Church to steal this doctrine of the Rapture. As soon as he could, also in 50 A.D., Paul wrote 2 Thessalonians to set the Church back on track. He rebuts a lying doctrine, introduced "by spirit (false implied) or by word or by letter", that the Day of the Lord had already come.

> [1] *Now, brethren, concerning the coming of our Lord Jesus Christ and our gathering together to Him, we ask you,*
> [2] *not to be soon shaken in mind or troubled, either by spirit or by word or by letter, as if from us, as though the day of Christ had come.*
> [3] *Let no one deceive you by any means;* **for that**

> *Day will not come unless the falling away comes first, and the man of sin is revealed, the son of perdition,*
> [4] *who opposes and exalts himself above all that is called God or that is worshiped, so that he sits as God in the temple of God, showing himself that he is God.*
>
>   2 Thessalonians 2:1-4 (emphasis added)

After Paul corrected the Church in the second letter, the Rapture became "settled doctrine" and prevailed as truth until the 4th century A.D. At that time, various false doctrines began to emerge that are still prevalent in the Church today.

Paul discussed the Rapture doctrine again in 56 A.D. In 1 Corinthians 15 he expounds in a scholarly way on the general topic of resurrection. First, he waxes eloquent on the subject of Our Risen Lord. He then discusses the resurrection of the dead saints, building toward the end of the age to a great and thrilling mystery!

> [51] *Behold, I tell you a mystery: We shall not all sleep, but we shall all be changed—* [52] *in a moment, in the twinkling of an eye, at the last trumpet. For the trumpet will sound, and **the dead will be raised incorruptible, and we shall be changed.*** [53] *For this corruptible must put on incorruption, and this mortal must put on immortality.* [54] *So when this corruptible has put on incorruption, and this mortal has put on immortality, then shall be brought to pass the saying that is written: "Death is swallowed up in victory".*
>
>   1 Corinthians 15:51-54 (emphasis added)

(Again, Paul uses the word "sleep" instead of the offensive

word "die" just as we use the term "passed away" today.)

> *¹ But concerning the times and the seasons, brethren, you have no need that I should write to you.² For you yourselves know perfectly that the day of the Lord so comes as a thief in the night.³ For when they say, "Peace and safety!" then sudden destruction comes upon them, as labor pains upon a pregnant woman. And they shall not escape.⁴ But you, brethren, are not in darkness, so that this Day should not overtake you as a thief.*
>
> *⁹ For God did not appoint us to wrath, but to obtain salvation through our Lord Jesus Christ, ¹⁰ who died for us, that whether we wake or sleep, we should live together with Him.*
>
> 1 Thessalonians 5:1-4; 9-10 (emphasis added)

I take the view that the Olivet Discourse (Matthew 24 and 25) is addressed to the Jews and not the Church.

1. In verse 3 the disciples ask Jesus: "What will be the sign of your coming, and of the end of the age?" The word "coming" is "parousia" in Greek, meaning coming as a king, which occurs at the end of the Tribulation.

2. Verses 5-9 are parallels to the four horsemen: false christ, war, famine, death. The horsemen ride out after the Rapture of the Church.

3. Verse 13 "He who endures to the end shall be saved". This is to the Jews. The Church is not saved by enduring, but by confessing Jesus is Lord.

4. Verse 15 prays against a flight on the Sabbath. A Christian may travel any distance he desires

on the Sabbath, an observant Jew may not.

Therefore I conclude that the passage, "You know not the day nor the hour", which Jesus uses repeatedly in the Olivet Discourse, is addressed to the Jews, not the Church. Furthermore, it is a reference to His second coming as a King. Why does no one know the day and the hour? Jesus Himself said He would shorten the days (Matthew 24:22). This might relate to a surprise attack on the Antichrist or his troops.

"REFERENCE SECOND COMING, NOT RAPTURE"
1. Matthew 24:36 – 36 "But of that day and hour no one knows, not even the angels of heaven, but My Father only.
2. Matthew 24:42 – 42 "Watch therefore, for you do not know what hour your Lord is coming".
3. Matthew 24:44 – 44 "Therefore you also be ready, for the Son of Man is coming at an hour you do not expect".
4. Matthew 25:13 – 13 "Watch therefore, for you know neither the day nor the hour in which the Son of Man is coming.

As I write this book, the call by Jesus to the Church to "Come up here" is only a few short years away. Revelation knowledge of this holy event is pouring out on the Church, by the Holy Spirit, all over the globe. Our spirits soar as this exciting time draws near...

> [7] *Let us be glad and rejoice and give Him glory, for the marriage of the Lamb has come, and **His wife has made herself ready.**[8] And to her it was granted to be arrayed in fine linen, clean and bright, for the fine linen is the righteous acts of the saints.*
>
> [9] *Then he said to me, Write: '**Blessed are those who are called to the marriage supper of the Lamb!**'" And he said to me, "These are the true sayings of God.*
>
> Revelation 19:7-9 (emphasis added)

Let us read what Tommy Hicks was shown in a vision of the Rapture in Winnipeg, Canada in 1967.

> *"I looked upon the earth, and the graves were opened and people from all over the world, the saints of all ages, seemed to be rising...It was so marvelous. But as this body suddenly began to form, and take shape again, in the form of this mighty giant, it was arrayed in the most beautiful gorgeous white. Its garments were without spot or wrinkle as its body began to form, suddenly from the heavens above, the Lord Jesus came, and became the head, and I heard another clap of thunder that said, "This is my beloved bride for whom I have waited. She will come forth even tried by fire. This is she that I have loved from the beginning of time".*

But when will the Church be Raptured?

It is our view that the Rapture is pre-tribulation. God did not appoint the Church to wrath. Furthermore, the Angel Gabriel specifically told Daniel the prophet that the seven year Tribulation was a time when God would deal with the Jews. Another name for the Tribulation is "Daniel's 70th Week". Remember that the Church is not mentioned in the Old Testament, it was a hidden mystery. Therefore, when Gabriel says, "your people and your holy city", he is referring to the Jews.

> [24] *"Seventy weeks are determined*
> *For your people and for your holy city.."*.
>
> Daniel 9:24

The chart below shows scripture reference comparing the Rapture of the church and the second coming of Christ.

	Rapture	SECOND COMING
1.	Meet the Lord in the air 1 Thessalonians 4:17	The Lord will come to earth Zechariah 14:4
2.	Only believers see Him Matthew 23:29	Every eye will see Him Revelation 1:17
3.	Takes the Church with Him to heaven John 14:3	Brings the Church with Him from heaven Jude 14, 15
4.	Comes to save the Church Luke 21:26	Comes to save the Jews Joel 3:16
5.	After the Rapture, the Tribulation begins Revelation 4:1	After the Second Coming, the Millennium begins Revelation 20:1-5

THE MARRIAGE SUPPER OF THE LAMB

When Jesus lived on earth, it was a Jewish custom for the

bride to come, after the marriage, and live in her father-in-law's home. Before the wedding, the groom was required to add on to the father's house a suitable dwelling place. Jesus is presently fulfilling the role of our Bridegroom.

> ² *In My Father's house are many mansions; if it were not so, I would have told you. **I go to prepare a place for you.** ³ And if I go and prepare a place for you, **I will come again and receive you to Myself;** that where I am, there you may be also.*
>
> John 14:2, 3 (emphasis added)

The Apostle Paul explained further that we are united with Jesus in a spiritual union or marriage.

> ²⁴ *Therefore, just as the church is subject to Christ,..".*
>
> ²⁷ *that He might present her to Himself a glorious church, not having spot or wrinkle or any such thing, but that she should be holy and without blemish.*
>
> ³⁰ *For we are members of His body, of His flesh and of His bones. ³¹ For this reason a man shall leave his father and mother and be joined to his wife, **and the two shall become one flesh.** ³² **This is a great mystery, but I speak concerning Christ and the church.***
>
> Ephesians 5:24, 27, 30–32 (emphasis added)

In the following passage the Bible clearly states that while the nations are being judged on earth we will receive our reward in heaven (see Chapter 10 in this book).

> ¹⁷ *saying:*
> *"We give You thanks, O Lord God Almighty, The One who is and who was and who is to come, Because You have taken Your great power and*

reigned.

[18] *The nations were angry, and Your wrath has come, And the time of the dead, that they should be judged,* **And that You should reward Your servants the prophets and the saints, And those who fear Your name,** *small and great,..."*

Revelation 11:17-18 (emphasis added)

Will the Church rule the earth in the Millennium, as mayors, governors and presidents, or is our reign of a spiritual nature? I take the view that it is the Jews that rule the earth; the Church will co-reign with Jesus over the universe. David Baron adopts that point of view:

> *"The Mission of the Church is to evangelize the world with a view to the gathering in of individuals out of all nations into its fold, but is reserved for restored and converted Israel as a nation to bring the nations to the knowledge of their glorious Messiah and King, and bring universal blessing to the world".*[12]

The eternality of this Jewish call is expressed to Daniel the Prophet in the following beautiful passage.

> [18] *"But the saints of the Most High shall receive the kingdom, and possess the kingdom forever, even forever and ever".*

Daniel 7:18

However, the eternal destiny of the Church is much loftier, the highest call human beings will ever achieve. We are married to Jesus and we are NOT unequally yoked (For God would not violate His own written word by giving Jesus an unequally yoked bride - see 2 Corinthians 6:14).

Jesus, speaking to Nicodemus, said this: "Except a man

be born again, he cannot see the kingdom of God" John 3:3. The words "born again" are in Greek "gennethe anothen". They literally mean "born from above". When we accept Jesus as our Savior and Lord and believe God raised Him from the dead, the Holy Spirit enters our spirit, we are born again and betrothed to Jesus.

There are only a finite number of people who will be in this glorious bridal party, as Paul explains.

> *[25] For I do not desire, brethren, that you should be ignorant of this mystery, lest you should be wise in your own opinion, that blindness in part has happened to Israel until the **fullness of the Gentiles** has come in.*
>
> Romans 11:25 (emphasis added)

We take the view that somewhere on earth a final Gentile will come to the Lord, and then the command goes forth: "Come up here".

> *[1] After these things I looked, and behold, a door standing open in heaven.*
> *And the first voice which I heard was like a trumpet speaking with me, saying,*
> *"Come up here, and I will show you things which must take place after this".*
>
> Revelation 4:1

After that point the Church Age is closed.

Those who come to Jesus during the Tribulation, (including Tribulation martyrs) have a wonderful future, but they are not the Bride of Christ.

THE MILLENNIAL REIGN OF JESUS

We, the Bride of Christ, will rule out of Heavenly Jerusalem.

Heavenly Jerusalem will be connected to earthly Jerusalem during the Millennial Reign. Picture it as connected by a stairway, or a bridge. Remember the name "Jerusalem" is plural in the Hebrew language, because there are two of them, heavenly Jerusalem and earthly Jerusalem. The Word says:

> *3 Jerusalem is built*
> *As a city that is compact together,*
>
> Psalm 122:3

In his Companion Bible E. W. Bullinger[13] defines the word "compact" - (compact = coupled together, as by a bridge), page 846.

We the Body of Christ, will rule over the continually expanding universe with the Lord Jesus forever. The 1,000 year Millennium will be a transitional time, with some features similar to eternity.

1. Satan will be bound - **Revelation 20:1,2 –** *1 Then I saw an angel coming down from heaven, having the key to the bottomless pit and a great chain in his hand. 2 He laid hold of the dragon, that serpent of old, who is the Devil and Satan, and bound him for a thousand years;*

2. The world will be ruled as a theocracy from the city of Jerusalem and men will learn war no more. **Isaiah 2:2-4 –** *2 Now it shall come to pass in the latter days That the mountain of the Lord's house Shall be established on the top of the mountains, And shall be exalted above the hills; And all nations shall flow to it. 3 Many people shall come and say, "Come, and let us go up to the mountain of the Lord, To the house of the God of Jacob; He will teach us His ways, And we shall walk in His paths". For out of Zion shall go forth the law, And the word of the Lord from Jerusalem. 4 He*

shall judge between the nations, And rebuke many people; They shall beat their swords into plowshares, And their spears into pruning hooks; Nation shall not lift up sword against nation, Neither shall they learn war anymore.

3. All nations (of earthly people) will be required to send their leaders to Jerusalem to honor Jesus annually at the Feast of Tabernacles. **Zechariah 14:16-18** - Zechariah 14:16-18 – *[16] And it shall come to pass that everyone who is left of all the nations which came against Jerusalem shall go up from year to year to worship the King, the Lord of hosts, and to keep the Feast of Tabernacles. [17] And it shall be that whichever of the families of the earth do not come up to Jerusalem to worship the King, the Lord of hosts, on them there will be no rain. [18] If the family of Egypt will not come up and enter in, they shall have no rain; they shall receive the plague with which the Lord strikes the nations who do not come up to keep the Feast of Tabernacles.*

THE TRANSITION TO ETERNITY

How blessed we will be as citizens of heavenly Jerusalem. We will be in a city hovering over earthly Jerusalem, "where the action is".

The Apostle Peter shows us the transition from the Millennium (Day of the Lord) to eternity (Day of God).

[10] But the day of the Lord will come as a thief in the night, in which the heavens will pass away with a great noise, and the elements will melt with fervent heat; both the earth and the works that are in it will be burned up. [11] Therefore, since all these things will be dissolved, what manner of persons

> *ought you to be in holy conduct and godliness,* ^{12}
> *looking for and hastening the coming of the **day**
> **of God,** because of which the heavens will be
> dissolved, being on fire, and the elements will melt
> with fervent heat?* ^{13} *Nevertheless we, according
> to His promise,* **look for new heavens and a
> new earth in which righteousness dwells.**
> 2 Peter 3:10-13 (emphasis added)

Scholars disagree as to whether just the surface of the earth or the whole planet will burn up at the end of the Millennium. Here is Clarence Larkin's[14] view:

> "...a careful study of the Scriptures will show us that what is to happen is, that this present earth, and the atmosphere surrounding it, is to be Renovated by Fire, so that its exterior surface shall be completely changed, and all that sin has brought into existence, such as thorns and thistles, disease germs, insect pests, and all viruses or plagues shall be destroyed and the atmosphere purified and forever freed from evil spirits and destructive agencies".

At this point our home, New Jerusalem (which had been hovering over the earth like a chandelier during the Millennium) will come and rest on the earth. Since there will then be "no more sea" (Revelation 21:1), possibly New Jerusalem will sit in the area where the Mediterranean Sea is now.

> ^{17} *"For behold, I create new heavens and a new
> earth; And the former shall not be remembered or
> come to mind.*
> Isaiah 65:17

> ^{22} *"For as the new heavens and the new earth*

Which I will make shall remain before Me", says
the Lord,
"So shall your descendants and your name
remain.
[23] *And it shall come to pass*
That from one New Moon to another,
And from one Sabbath to another,
All flesh shall come to worship before Me", says
the Lord.

Isaiah 66:22-23

We, the Body of Christ, will reign over the universe with Jesus as kings and priests forever.

CHAPTER 9

THE TEN KINGS
THAT
RULE THE WORLD

The belief that this present age would conclude with ten kings ruling the earth has been accepted by Bible scholars since antiquity. Daniel first alluded to the ten kings in the book of Daniel, written about 600 BC. They are the ten toes in Nebuchadnezzar's image in Daniel 2. Seven hundred years later, John expounded on them in Revelation. They are pictured here as the ten horns (Revelation 12:3; 13:1). Let us unveil eight of the ten kings, which I believe Scripture clearly identifies. Before we begin, it is important to understand that to Jehovah, Israel is the center of the earth (Ezekiel 5:5) All of human history revolves around this Holy Land. In the end, whoever rules Jerusalem will rule the world.

To understand who the ten kings are, we must answer this question:

Who are the seven kingdoms that have oppressed Israel throughout history?

Below is a key to help you memorize the answer.

Key – 7 Gentile Kingdoms

Every Ancient Biblical Message-Promise God Reveals Rightly

(Memorize the phrase and use this key to remember
the name of the seven kingdoms.)

Egypt, Assyria, Babylon, Medo-Persia, Greece, Rome, Revived Rome

(You will learn more from this book if you commit the key to memory.)

Notice in the following Scriptures that the ten horns (kings) **come out of the seven heads** (kingdoms that oppressed Israel).

Satan is ... *a great fiery red dragon **having seven heads and ten horns,** and **seven diadems** on his heads* Revelation 12:3 (emphasis added).

Antichrist is ...*a beast rising up out of the sea, **having seven heads and ten horns,** and on his horns **ten crowns**...* Revelation 13:1 (emphasis added).

Since the ten horns are on the seven heads, we can safely conclude: the ten kings come out of the seven heads. The seven heads are: Egypt, Assyria, Babylon, Medo-Persia, Greece, Rome and Revived Rome.

The ten horns are explained in Revelation 17:

[12] *"The ten horns which you saw are ten kings who*

have received no kingdom as yet, **but they receive authority for one hour as kings with the beast.** [13] *These are of one mind, and they will give their power and authority to the beast".*
Revelation 17:12-13 (emphasis added)

The ten kings are leaders of the revived Roman Empire. They only rule the world during Antichrist's reign, the second half of the Tribulation.

Four of the above nations also ruled and/or dominated Jerusalem. They are Iraq, Iran, Greece and Rome.

The book of Daniel defines their role in very great detail in several images. We see them described as the four metals in Nebuchadnezzar's image in Daniel 2, and the four great beasts of Daniel 7. Compare the image in Daniel 2 with the great beasts of Daniel 7 and the countries each represents.

COUNTRY	NEBUCHADNEZZAR'S IMAGE (DANIEL 2)	FOUR GREAT BEASTS (DANIEL 7)	RAM & THE GOAT (DANIEL 8)
Babylon (Iraq)	Head — Gold —	Lion	
Medo-Persia (Iran)	Chest and Arms — Silver —	Bear	Ram
Greece	Belly and Thighs — Bronze —	Leopard	Goat
Rome ——— Revived Rome	Legs — Iron — ———— Feet and Toes — Iron and Clay —	Dreadful Beast	

These four nations are also represented by the four chariots of Zechariah and the four horsemen of Revelation 6. They will reap great judgment for their treatment of God's chosen people, the Jews. But before they are judged, they will again deal severe body blows to believers and Jews who are on the earth during the Tribulation. To get an overview of things to come, let us look more closely at the feet of iron and clay, and then the dreadful beast.

The ten toes of iron and clay represent the ten final kings:

> [41] *Whereas you saw the feet and toes, partly of potter's clay and partly of iron,* **the kingdom shall be divided;** *yet the strength of the iron shall be in it, just as you saw the iron mixed with ceramic clay.* [42] *And as the toes of the feet were partly of iron and partly of clay, so the kingdom shall be partly strong and partly fragile.* [43] *As you saw* **iron mixed with ceramic clay,** *they will mingle with the seed of men; but* **they will not adhere to one another,** *just as iron does not mix with clay.*
>
> Daniel 2:41-43 (emphasis added)

"The kingdom shall be divided" Daniel 2:41, but *"they will not adhere to one another",* Daniel 2:43.

The iron in the feet and toes must be the revived Roman Empire. The legs of iron were the ancient Roman Empire. The iron in the feet represents the so-called "socialist democracies" in the European Union.

The "feet" of iron and clay rule in the first 3 1/2 years of the Tribulation. The European Union probably dominates the world, and it has many members. The clay is Islam. **The "toes" of iron and clay** are the ten kings. They only rule during the second 3 1/2 years of the Tribulation with the beast. They receive authority for one hour (Revelation 17:12).

The clay, or Islam, is described in the King James Version as "partly broken". (Daniel 2:42). This may symbolize the lack of unity between the Shi'ite and Sunni Muslims, or it may illustrate that the Antichrist has to "break" three Islamic nations, Egypt, Libya, and Ethiopia, before they will follow him (Daniel 11:43).

SUBSTANCE	REPRESENTS	DANIEL 2:42
Iron	"Socialist Democracies" Revived Roman Empire/ Apostate Church	Strong
Clay	Dictatorship/Islam	Broken (KJV)

THE FEET OF IRON AND CLAY:

The Christianity (feet of iron), which aligns itself with Islam (feet of clay), is in fact the Apostate Church. Even in apostasy, they cannot successfully mix their doctrine with the beliefs of the Muslims. Thus, as we shall see in Chapter 11 of this book, the Apostate Church is burned by fire 3 1/2 years into the Tribulation. The Apostate Church is headquartered in Rome and is destroyed by the ten kings.

Now we shall consider the dreadful beast.

> [7] *After this I saw in the night visions, and behold, a fourth beast, dreadful and terrible, exceedingly strong. It had huge iron teeth; it was devouring, breaking in pieces, and trampling the residue with its feet. It was different from all the beasts that were before it, **and it had ten horns.***
>
> Daniel 7:7 (emphasis added)

It is my view that the Union for the Mediterranean is emerging as the dreadful beast, even as I write this book. This union includes both the European Union and the Islamic nations of North Africa and the Middle East.

Western Kings	Eastern Kings
Rome (Italy)	Assyria (Turkey)
Greece	Babylon (Iraq)
Libya	Medo-Persia (Iran)
Egypt	Ethiopia

Daniel continues the description.

> [23] *"Thus he said:*
>
> *'The fourth beast shall be*
> *A fourth kingdom on earth,*
> *Which shall be different from all other kingdoms,*
> *And **shall devour the whole earth,***
> *Trample it and break it in pieces.*
> [24] *The ten horns are ten kings*
> ***Who shall arise from this kingdom.***
> *And another shall rise after them;*

He shall be different from the first ones,
And ***shall subdue three kings.***

Daniel 7:23-24 (emphasis added)

The Bible does not say that the ten kings will be a confederation of ten nations, as some have taught. **Rather, the Bible says ten kings "shall arise" from the fourth kingdom** (Daniel 7:24). This kingdom is "different" from all other kingdoms. **Notice that the total number of kings in the fourth kingdom is not given in the Bible. There are 46 nations in the "Union for the Mediterranean", but only ten will rule with Antichrist.**

Three of these kings will be "subdued" mid-Tribulation. Then "another shall arise after them", the Antichrist. He is not one of the original ten kings. Let us direct our attention to the three kings who need to be subdued. It is my view that the Shi'ite Antichrist subdues three Sunni nations during the first half of the Tribulation.

However, the Antichrist will not solidify his power grab until mid-Tribulation. The length of his reign of terror is only 42 months (Revelation 13:5).

Daniel 11 describes the events that unfold during the first half of the Tribulation, as the Antichrist seizes power and subdues three Kings:

> [40] *At the time of the end the king of the South (Egypt) shall attack him (Antichrist); and the king of the North (Antichrist) shall come against him (Egypt) like a whirlwind, with chariots, horsemen, and with many ships; and he shall enter the countries, overwhelm them, and pass through. [41] He (Antichrist) shall also enter the Glorious Land (Israel), and many countries shall be overthrown; but these shall escape from his hand: Edom, Moab, and the prominent people*

of Ammon (Jordan). [42] He shall stretch out his hand against the countries, and the land of Egypt shall not escape. [43] He shall have power over the treasures of gold and silver, and over all the precious things of Egypt; also the Libyans and Ethiopians shall follow at his heels.

Daniel 11:40-43

(parenthesis author's interpretation)

Therefore, we conclude that the three kings who are coerced into following Antichrist are Egypt, Ethiopia and Libya. It is our unproven theory that these staunch Sunni Islamic states, which have pledged themselves to Allah, will not appreciate the Antichrist's demand that they now worship him.

Let us now sift through the information we have compiled:

1. We wish to identify ten kings.

2. The ten toes on Nebuchadnezzar's image represent them. Since each foot has five toes, each half of the Roman Empire will represent five kings. We divide the kingdom at Israel. Geographically, five kings will reign from countries east of Israel; five kings will reign from countries west of Israel.

3. There will be Islamic dictatorships and "socialist [4]democracies" of the EU in both the west and the east. **This must be true because both feet are partly iron and partly clay** (Daniel 2:41-43).

4. Six of the kings are identified as: Egypt, Assyria, Babylon, Medo-Persia, Greece, and Rome.

5. Three kings must be subdued. They are: Egypt, Libya, and Ethiopia. (Biblical Ethiopia may include modern Sudan.)

Notice Egypt is mentioned in both lists.

Based on the above, I conclude that the Bible gives us eight of the ten kings who will rule at the end of the age. They are:

GEOGRAPHIC LOCATION	MODERN NATION	ANCIENT BIBLICAL NAME
WEST	Italy Greece Libya Egypt	Rome Greece Libya Egypt
EAST	Turkey Iraq Iran Ethiopia	Assyria Babylon Medo-Persia Ethiopia
*Author's Opinion		

In the interest of intellectual honesty, we must admit that Iran was not considered a part of the Roman Empire. The ancient Persian Empire was rather considered an antagonist of Rome. However, because it is one of the seven ancient empires (one of seven heads) out of which the ten horns come, I have included it.

The ancient Assyrian Empire included portions of Turkey, Syria, and Iraq. Since we have listed Iraq and Iran as two of the kings, we will focus here on Turkey and Syria. It is my view that Turkey will be one of the ten kings. Let us now consider the Antichrist, also from Assyria:

> [7] *...And another shall rise after them; he shall be different from the first ones,...*
>
> Daniel 7:24

This king, the Antichrist, will arise from the Assyrian Empire. (Micah 5:5-6) He will be from Syria, and he will ultimately rule the ten kings.

Of those eight kings, the destiny of at least six of their kingdoms is known. Iraq, Iran, Greece and Rome seem to be "goat nations". It appears that they do not enter the Millennial reign.

> [35] *Then the iron (Rome), the clay (Islam), the bronze (Greece), the silver (Iran), and the gold (Iraq) were crushed together, and became like chaff from the summer threshing floors; the wind carried them away so that no trace of them was found. And the stone that struck the image became a great mountain and filled the whole earth.*
>
> Daniel 2:35 (countries in parenthesis added)

We see similar terminology used by Asaph in Psalm 83, describing the judgment of the Islamic nations.

However, Egypt and Syria will remain, although Egypt will be depopulated for 40 years, possibly because of radiation from nuclear bombs (Ezekiel 29:12, 13). Egypt and Syria will enter the Millennium, as friends with Israel, which we are happy to report.

> [22] *And the Lord will strike Egypt, He will strike and heal it; they will return to the Lord, and He will be entreated by them and heal them.*
> [23] *In that day there will be a highway from Egypt to Assyria, and the Assyrian will come into Egypt and the Egyptian into Assyria, and the Egyptians will serve with the Assyrians.*

[24] In that day Israel will be one of three with Egypt and Assyria—a blessing in the midst of the land,

[25] whom the Lord of hosts shall bless, saying, "Blessed is Egypt My people, and Assyria the work of My hands, and Israel My inheritance.

Isaiah 19:22-25

What about America, the strong and righteous nation that has defended the poor and weak for so long? America is now in decline, due to immorality and government policies. Pastor John Kilpatrick, of the Bay of the Holy Spirit Revival, tells of this encouraging prophecy given by Dr. David Cho in Seattle, Washington in 1993.

The Word of the Lord: I have not forgotten America. I will pour out My Spirit, first in Pensacola. It will burn like a match head. It will spread and go over to the River of the Holy Spirit (Mississippi River). It will back up and go along the Gulf Coast a second time. It will go down the peninsula of Florida. It will go up the Eastern Seaboard, come across the Midwest, the Southwest and shoot out to the Northwest, and before My coming all America will be ablaze with the glory of God.

Read on to see what the Word of God has to say about the upcoming seven year Tribulation, also called "Daniel's seventieth week" (Daniel 9:27).

CHAPTER 10

THE TRIBULATION:
AN OVERVIEW

I t is the purpose of this chapter to provide a general explanation of the upcoming Tribulation. To understand each seal, trumpet, vial, plague and earthquake, the reader is encouraged to consult and study the Word of God. It is the view of many scholars that the book of Revelation is, for the most part, in chronological order. **God is the Perfect Father; He is not trying to confuse His people!**

The next two pages contain a chart that will assist the reader in understanding the Tribulation.

The first 3 ¹/₂ years of the Tribulation are called the

EVENT	WRATH OF THE LAMB
WILL BEGIN*	Probably in September - October
DURATION	3 1/2 Years Revelation 11:3
DISCUSSED IN	Revelation Chapters 6 - 9 and 11:15
AREA AFFECTED	1/3 of the Earth [Area of 10 Kings plus Russia*] Revelation 8:7 - 12; 9:18
FIRST EVENT	The 4 horsemen released Revelation 6:1 - 8
THIRD HEAVEN SEEN ON EARTH	An open heaven - God's throne seen Revelation 6:14 - 16
EVENTS INCLUDE	7 Seals, 7 Trumpets Revelation Chapters 6 - 10
JUDGMENTS ORDERED BY	Jesus Revelation 6:16
ROLE OF EUPHRATES RIVER	4 Angels released with 200 million man army 6th trumpet Revelation 9:13 - 16
PRIMARY PREACHERS IN THE ERA	Elijah, another witness and 144,000 Jewish witnesses Revelation 7:5 - 8; 11:3
CULMINATES IN	3 Woes and End of Church Age Revelation 11:15, 18 1st Woe Rev. 9:2, 11 - 12 2nd Woe Rev. 9:14, 11:7, 14 3rd Woe Rev. 12:12
* denotes author's opinion	

EVENT	WRATH OF JEHOVAH
Will Begin*	Probably in March - April
Duration	3 1/2 Years Revelation 13:5
Discussed In	Revelation Chapters 14 - 16 and 18
Area Affected	Entire World Revelation 13:3; 13:7 Zechariah 12:3; Daniel 7:23 Jeremiah 25:26; Joel 3:2
First Event	Antichrist seizes Jerusalem Revelation 11:7; Daniel 11:41a, 45
Third Heaven Seen On Earth	An open heaven God's tabernacle and ark seen Revelation 11:19; 13:6; 15:5
Events Include	7 Vials (also called bowls) Revelation Chapters 15 & 16
Judgments Ordered By	God the Father Revelation 15:1 and 16:1
Role of Euphrates River	River dries up Kings of the east march forth 6th Vial - Revelation 16:12
Primary Preachers In The Era	Angels and Jesus Himself Revelation 14:6-13; 16:15
Culminates In	Jesus returns with the saints on Mt. Olive Revelation 19:11 - 14; Isaiah 52:7; Nahum 1:15; Zechariah 14:4; Jude 14,15
* denotes author's opinion	

"Wrath of the Lamb". The judgments (except the spread of Islam) are confined to Israel's enemies. Notice that those judgments come to a third part of the earth:

> [7] ...the third part of the trees was burned up...
> [8] ...the third part of the sea became blood...
> [9] ...the third part of the creatures which were in the sea, and had life died...
> [10] ...a great star from heaven...fell upon the third part of the rivers...
>
> Revelation 8:7-10 KJV

> [12]...the day shone not for a third part of it (the earth)...
>
> Revelation 8:12 KJV
> (parenthesis author's opinion)

> [18]By these was the third part of men killed,...
>
> Revelation 9:18 KJV

Many scholars agree that these are not judgments on a literal third of human beings and nature. Since this is the Wrath of the Lamb (Jesus), we see this as a destruction on *some* trees, *some* animals and *some* human beings who occupy one third of planet earth. Remember that Jesus judges those who mistreat the Jews.

> [40]"...inasmuch as you did it to one of the least of these My brethren, you did it to Me".
>
> Matthew 25:40

See Micah 5:3 for a better understanding of the word "brethren".

The European Union only represents one fourth of the world. But the Wrath of the Lamb will judge "a third part" of the world. Thus we include Russia in these judgments, just as we included Russia in the famine that followed the

Ezekiel War (see page 92). Although Russia is not one of the seven enemies of Israel, historically their record against Israel has been abysmal. Under the Czars in the 1800's there were many pogroms (massacres of Jews and destruction of their property) in Russia. Beginning in 1881, the May Laws herded Jews into Russian ghettos. After the Communists took control in 1917, the Jews were trapped in this hostile land. When the Jewish state was founded in 1948, Russian Jews desired to go home. The Communists forbade it.

Of course, God had foreseen all of this, as Isaiah had prophesied two millennia earlier. The Jews would return to Israel freely from the East and West; but He would have to order the North (Russia) to give them up. God fulfilled this prophecy when He sovereignly dismantled Soviet Communism in 1989.

> [5] *Fear not, for I am with you; I will bring your descendants from the east, And gather you from the west;*
> [6] **I will say to the north, "Give them up!..."**
>   Isaiah 43:5, 6 (emphasis added)

Therefore, we include Russia in the third of the earth that will be judged during the Wrath of the Lamb. This era will conclude with the last three trumpets, which are also called the "three woes".

I see the woes, exclamations of grief, as relating to demonic invasion into earthly affairs:

1. First woe - the release of Apollyon, a Grecian evil prince

2. Second woe - the release of the four evil demon princes of Egypt, Assyria, Iraq and Iran

3. Third woe - the casting of Satan, the prince of the power of the air, to earth

THE FIRST WOE (Revelation 8:13; 9:1–12)

The king of the bottomless pit is released with his hordes to torment men for five months. Both the Hebrew name, Abaddon, and the Greek name, Apollyon, of this evil spirit are given. He is the demon who may soon indwell the Antichrist. Is it possible that he is the ancient prince of Greece spoken of in Daniel 10:20? Since the Antichrist will be a Syrian Greek, (see page 40) I would not be surprised to see this Grecian demon possessing him.

I expect that Apollyon, and not Satan, indwells the Antichrist because of the following:

1. Apollyon is called "the angel of the bottomless pit" (Revelation 9:11).

2. Antichrist is referred to as "the beast from the bottomless pit" (Revelation 11:7; 17:8).

3. Apollyon is referred to as having ascended out of the bottomless pit (Revelation 9:2,11); Antichrist is referred to as having ascended out of the bottomless pit (Revelation 17:8).

4. Antichrist and Satan are seen as separate entities throughout Revelation (Revelation 13:4; 16:13; 19:20; 20:2).

5. Apollyon is known in ancient Jewish writings and is sometimes referred to as Asmodeus, the prince of demons.

THE SECOND WOE (Revelation 9:12–19; 11:7–14)

The second woe includes the release of the four evil angels bound at the Euphrates River and the murder of the two witnesses by the Antichrist, after which he seizes Jerusalem. The two witnesses had ordered plagues and drought against Israel's enemies. The evil world rejoices when they're slain, and sends each other gifts. Antichrist's stellar rise to fame is global! For the first time since Alexander the Great, one man claims the right to rule the world.

But who are the four evil angels who were released from the Euphrates? The six ancient enemies of Israel were each led by an evil angel. The Roman evil angel is the driving force behind the European Union. The Greek evil angel, Apollyon, could be the spirit that indwells the Antichrist. Where are the evil angels who ruled ancient Egypt, Assyria, Babylon, and Medo-Persia? Could it be that they are still bound at the great river?

During the second woe, the order goes out:

[14] ... *"Release the four angels that are bound at the great river Euphrates".*

Revelation 9:14

Is it possible that these are the four ancient evil spirits that ruled Egypt, Assyria, Babylon and Medo-Persia? These angels gather an army of 200 million horsemen by whom were killed *"the third part of mankind..."* (Revelation 9:18 KJV). Biblical evidence that this is an Islamic army is compelling.

1. Chronologically, we are approaching the middle of the Tribulation Period. The European Union still rules the world (Daniel 7:7), but the Islamic Antichrist will soon take over (Daniel 7:8). The army of Revelation 9:16 is being assembled to defeat the European Union and Russia and China.

2. The assignment of this army is *"...to slay the third part of men"* Revelation 9:15 KJV. As we have

already discussed, the Revived Roman Empire and Russia comprise a third part of men.

3. John heard the total number of men in this army, "200 million". I believe this army, led by the Shiite Antichrist, is not initially that large or powerful. His access to Iran's nuclear weapons will be a persuasive tool. He may also possess other weapons of mass destruction. As the Antichrist vanquishes Sunni nations, or makes pacts and truces with them, the size of his army will increase. (For example, Indonesia alone has over 50 million men available for military service). Only after the Antichrist defeats Egypt, Libya and Ethiopia, does this army contain 200 million men.

4. It is my view that the 200 million man army of Revelation 9:16 is not an Oriental army. I believe this for several reasons:

    a. The book of Revelation is in chronological order. The Chinese army appears in Revelation 16, the second half of the Tribulation.

    b. Furthermore, the army from the east passes over the dried riverbed of the Euphrates in Revelation 16:12. This river bed is not dry during the first half of the tribulation. Notice that John sees the Euphrates River in Revelation 9:14, and makes no mention of it being "dry". Therefore it becomes dry in relation to the 6th bowl judgment at the very end of the Tribulation (Revelation 16:12).

    c. The prophet Daniel describes Antichrist's army as "overwhelming" in Daniel 11:40

No wonder John says of Antichrist's 200 million man army in Revelation 13:4:

> *⁴ "Who is like the beast. Who is able to make war with him?"*

The two witnesses who are killed (Revelation 11:7) are believed by most scholars to be Enoch and Elijah, who have never died (Hebrews 9:27), or Elijah and Moses. For 3 1/2 years they had discipled and led 144,000 Messianic Jewish evangelists. After the Rapture, the Jews took over the task of winning the world to Jesus, (Revelation 11:7–12). The 144,000 witnesses must also be Raptured midway through the Tribulation since they are seen in heaven in Revelation 14:1 when the Wrath of Jehovah begins.

And so in the middle of the Tribulation, as referenced in the prologue, the Mystery of God will be finished. We believe the words *"there should be time no longer"* refers to the end of the sixth millennium:

> *⁶ And sware by him that liveth for ever and ever, who created heaven, and the things that therein are, and the earth, and the things that therein are, and the sea, and the things which are therein, **that there should be time no longer:***
> *⁷ But in the days of the voice of the seventh angel, when he shall begin to sound, **the mystery of God should be finished,** as he hath declared to his servants the prophets.*
>   Revelation 10:6-7 KJV (emphasis added)

The Mystery of God includes the assignment of the Church to preach to the principalities and powers in the heavens:

> *⁹ and to make all see what is the fellowship of the mystery, which from the beginning of the ages*

*has been hidden in God who created all things through Jesus Christ; ^{10} to the intent that now **the manifold wisdom of God might be made known by the church to the principalities and powers in the heavenly places.***

Ephesians 3:9-10 (emphasis added)

The seventh trumpet, also called the third woe, will topple Satan and his minions from the heavenlies.

^{7} *And war broke out in heaven: Michael and his angels fought with the dragon; and the dragon and his angels fought, ^{8} but they did not prevail, not was a place found for them in heaven any longer. ^{9} So the great dragon was cast out, that serpent of old, called the Devil and Satan, who deceives the whole world; he was cast to the earth, and his angels were cast out with him.*

^{12} *Therefore rejoice, O heavens, and you who dwell in them! Woe to the inhabitants of the earth and the sea! **For the devil has come down to you,** having great wrath, because he knows he has a short time.*

Revelation 12:7-9, 12 (emphasis added)

[handwritten margin note: what millennium are we in?]

And so, like falling dominoes, the mid-Tribulation events include:

1. The end of the Wrath of the Lamb and the sixth millennium.

2. The death of Elijah and the other witness and the Rapture of the 144,000 witnesses.

3. The casting of Satan and his forces to earth.

4. The reward of the saints in heaven (Revelation 11:18).

5. The flight of the Messianic Jews from Israel to Petra for 3 ¹/₂ years (Revelation 12:6 & 14).

6. The initiation of the Wrath of Jehovah, which begins with an open heaven:

¹⁷ *Saying, "We give thee thanks, O Lord God Almighty, which art, and wast, and art to come; because* **thou hast taken to thee thy great power , and hast reigned.**

¹⁸ *And the nations were angry, and* **thy wrath is come,** *and the time of the dead, that they should be judged, and that thou shouldest give reward unto thy servants the prophets, and to the saints, and them that fear thy name, small and great;* **and shouldest destroy them which destroy the earth".**

¹⁹ **And the temple of God was opened in heaven,** *and there was seen in his temple the ark of his testament...*
            Revelation 11:17-19 KJV (emphasis added)

[NOTE: "Thou has taken to thee thy power and hast reigned..". "Hast reigned" in the Greek is in the ingressive first aorist active indicative tense, which implies a momentary, completed act. It would be more accurately translated *"Thou hast taken to thee thy great power and* **begun to reign"**. In other words, man's lease on planet earth has expired, and God has taken over.]

It is my view that the words "*...there should be time no longer"* (Revelation 10:6 KJV) mean that the 6,000 years of man's dominion over planet earth are finished (see page 21). Notice this prophecy is fulfilled in Chapter 11.

¹⁵ *Then the seventh angel sounded: And there were*

*loud voices in heaven, saying, **"The kingdoms of this world have become the kingdoms of our Lord** and of His Christ, and He shall reign forever and ever!"***

Revelation 11:15 (emphasis added)

Who is the Mighty Angel of Revelation 10 who prophesies the end of the sixth millennium, and the beginning of the seventh day, the Day of the Lord? Many authors identify the Mighty Angel as Jesus Himself. I concur for the reasons found in the chart on the next page:

Mighty Angel of Revelation	Scriptural References
1. He is clothed with a cloud. (Revelation 10:1)	"son of man, coming with the clouds..". Daniel 7:13 "...a cloud received Him..". Acts 1:9
2, A rainbow was on his head. (Revelation 10:1)	In the Bible, the rainbow is always associated with Deity. Revelation 4:2,3
3. His face was like the sun. (Revelation 10:1)	"His face shone like the sun..". Matthew 17:2b
4. He had a little book. (Revelation 10:2)	In Revelation 5:7 Jesus held a "book" (Strong's 975). Now He holds a "small book" (Strong's 974). The book is smaller (maybe because half of the judgments are completed).
5. The angel says, "And I will give power to my two witnesses..". (Revelation 11:3)	The angel refers to Elijah and the other witness as my two witnesses. They teach that Jesus is Messiah; therefore, they are His two witnesses. Revelation 11:3-12

And so, as I have just stated, Jesus (the Mighty Angel) prophesies the end of the sixth millennium in Revelation 10:6. This prophecy is then fulfilled in Revelation 11:15.

God never does anything unless He prophesies it first (Amos 3:7).

Finally, after 6,000 years of human history, mankind's rule on planet earth is concluded. The Day of the Lord, foretold by every Old Testament prophet, begins with three and a half years of Jehovah's Wrath. Concurrently, the saints in heaven receive their reward.

THE THIRD WOE

The third woe is the casting of Satan and his minions from the second heaven to the earth. It is the momentous event that winds up the sixth millennium and signals the beginning of the Day of the Lord.

> [9] *So the great dragon was cast out, that serpent of old, called the Devil and Satan, who deceives the whole world;* **he was cast to the earth, and his angels were cast out with him.**
>
> [10] *Then I heard a loud voice saying in heaven, "Now salvation and strength, and the kingdom of our God, and the power of His Christ have come,* **for the accuser of our brethren, who accused them before our God day and night, has been cast down.**
>
> [12] *"Therefore rejoice, O heavens, and you who dwell in them!* Woe *to the inhabitants of the earth and the sea!* **For the devil has come down to you,** *having great wrath, because he knows that he has a short time".*
>
> Revelation 12:9-10, 12 (emphasis added)

Let us review again the cataclysmic events at the end of this age, and the beginning of the Day of the Lord.

See the chart on the next page.

Mid-Tribulation Event	Supporting Scripture
1. End of Man's Dominion	"...in the days of the...seventh angel...the mystery of God would be finished..". Revelation 10:7
2. The beginning of the Day of the Lord	"The kingdoms of this world have become the kingdoms of our Lord and of His Christ..". Revelation 11:15 "O Lord God Almighty...You have taken your great power and reigned..". Revelation 11:17
3. The Wrath of God begins	"The nations were angry and your wrath has come..". Revelation 11:18
4. The saints are judged in heaven	"that they should be judged, and that you should reward your servants, the prophets and the saints..". Revelation 11:18
5. Rapture of Elijah and other witness	"...'Come up here,' and they ascended to heaven in a cloud..". Revelation 11:12
6. 144,000 witnesses are Raptured	"...a Lamb standing on Mount Zion, and with Him 144,000..". Revelation 14:1
7. An open heaven over the earth	"Then the temple of God was opened in heaven..". Revelation 11:19

Does the Church Age end with the Rapture, or with the burning of Rome midway through the Tribulation? It is a question of semantics. The "glorious Church" concludes at the Rapture. The "Apostate Church" endures 3 $1/2$ more years, until it is burned by the ten kings (see Chapter 11).

Notice that the open heaven, which initiates the second half of the Tribulation, is spoken of in Revelation 11:19 and then again in Revelation 15:5. It is my view that Revelation picks up the story in 15:5 where it left off at 11:19. In other words, the mid-Tribulation events of Chapters 12, 13 and 14:1-3 run concurrently (some of it taking place in the heavenlies) with Chapter 11.

When John resumes the narrative in 15:5 he explains the seven last plagues "...for in them the Wrath of God is complete" (Revelation 15:1). Thus we see the judgment is completed with an earthquake "...and the cities of the nations fell" (Revelation 16:19). Revelation 16:19 introduces Revelation 18, the judgment of Babylon. Jeremiah had already prophesied that the last king to be judged would be Antichrist, the king of Sheshach (Babylon), in Jeremiah 25:26.

It is my belief that the book of Revelation is, in essence, in chronological order. The exception is Chapter 17, a mid-Tribulation event. Why did John insert it near the end of the book?

CHAPTER 11

A TALE OF
TWO BURNED CITIES

As I just explained, for the most part, the events of Revelation are given in chronological order. The exception to this rule is Chapter 17, which deals with the burning of Rome. Rome is actually burned mid-Tribulation, in conjunction with the events of Revelation 11, 12 and 13. There are several possible reasons for inserting this mid-Tribulation catastrophe near the end of the Book of Revelation.

1. The Apostate Church, headquartered in Rome, is the harlot that sits on the seven-headed beast, the Antichrist (Revelation 17:3). The Antichrist is not introduced until Revelation 13. Therefore,

the woman sitting on the beast could not be identified until we know who the beast is.

2. The author wishes to compare the burning of Rome (Revelation 17) with the burning of Babylon (Revelation 18). Putting them in successive chapters helps to draw the analogy.
3. God is making a statement about His Holy City. The Babylonians burned Jerusalem in 586 B.C. The Romans burned Jerusalem in 70 A.D. Let this be a warning to every kingdom that comes against God's City: You will reap what you have sown!

The Bible interprets itself. When the Bible says "...Babylon the great is fallen..." (Revelation 18:2) there is no reason to believe that the Word is referring to any place on earth except Babylon.

According to the prophet Zechariah, prosperity will return to Shinar (Babylon) in the end times (Zechariah 5:5-11). Babylon is a city 55 miles south of Baghdad in Iraq.

Only in the last few years have we seen current events line up with this ancient prophecy. President Bush and the American military had attempted to bring forth a fledgling democracy in Iraq. Iraq has now become a client state of Iran, ruled by the Shiite majority. Its future wealth will flow from the god of mammon. The Bible clearly speaks of prosperity in Babylon during these end times. This wealth includes the buying and selling of:

> [12] *merchandise of gold and silver, precious stones and pearls, fine linen and purple, silk and scarlet, every kind of citron wood, every kind of object of most precious wood, bronze, iron, and marble;* [13] *and cinnamon and incense, fragrant oil and*

frankincense, wine and oil, fine flour and wheat, cattle and sheep, horses and chariots, and bodies and souls of men.

Revelation 18:12-13

How does a man sell his soul? By worshiping the beast or his image, or taking his mark or the number of his name.

[23] *...For your merchants were the great men of the earth, for by your sorcery all the nations were deceived.*

Revelation 18:23

According to Strong's Concordance, sorcery includes "drugs, incantations, charms, and magic". The occult practices of Babylon as well as Iraq's perennial hatred of the Jews will cause the Lord to pronounce a most severe judgment against her. In fact, after the Tribulation, no human being will ever inhabit Babylon again.

[49] *As Babylon has caused the slain of Israel to fall, So at Babylon the slain of all the earth shall fall.*

[62] *then you shall say, 'O Lord, You have spoken against this place to cut it off, so that none shall remain in it, neither man nor beast, but it shall be desolate forever'.*

Jeremiah 51:49, 62

I therefore conclude, as I have just explained, that Revelation 18 is not allegorical. It is to be believed as literal punishment on literal Babylon, beginning at the end of the Tribulation and continuing on in perpetuity.

Before we discuss Revelation 17, it will be helpful for the reader to consider the chart on the next page.

TWO BURNED CITIES		
COMPARE AND CONTRAST CHAPTERS 17 & 18		
CATEGORY	REVELATION 17 (VERSES)	REVELATION 18 (VERSES)
Geographic Area	Rome (9, 18)	Babylon (2, 10)
Primary Role of City	Religious Center of the Apostate Christian Church (Matthew 13:33)	Economic Center of Antichrist's Government (Zechariah 5:5 - 11; Revelation 18:15 - 16)
Judgment Announced	One of angels with seven bowls (1)	Another angel having great authority (1)
Judgment	City burned (16)	City burned (18)
Judged Because*	Burned Jerusalem in 70 A.D.	Burned Jerusalem in 586 B.C.
Burned By	Ten Kings (16)	God Himself (8)
When Burned	Mid Tribulation (12, 16)	End of Tribulation (Revelation 16:17 - 18)
Her Sins	Idolatry (2) Martyrs the Saints (6) Apostasy (Matthew 13:33)	Idolatry (3) Martyrs the Saints (24) Sells men (13) Sorcery (23) Illicit Commerce (Zechariah 5:8)
Attitude of Ten Kings	Hate Her (16)	Lament for her (9)
Length of Judgment	Not Given	Forever (21) (Isaiah 34:9 - 10) Jeremiah 51:58, 62)
*Denotes Author's Opinion		

Catholic ?

Let us now consider Revelation 17, the saga of "Mystery Babylon" (verse 5). Remembering that God is the Perfect Father, we know it is not His purpose to confuse us. As is His custom when He is revealing a mystery, He sends an interpreter, in this case an angel (verse 7). The woman in this chapter is the apostate Christian Church, as we shall soon see. Jesus had referred to her in a parable (remember leaven always represents evil when used in the word of God).

> [33] *Another parable He spoke to them: "The kingdom of heaven is like leaven, which a woman took and hid in three measures of meal till it was all leavened".*
>
> Matthew 13:33

David Baron explains what leaven is and how to stop its growth:

> **Leaven** *consists of a microscopic vegetable ferment, which is characterized chiefly by rapidity of its growth and diffusiveness, so that it permeates the whole lump into which it is put, and* **nothing is able to stop its growth except fire — a fit emblem, therefore, of corruption, of which it is the figure in every place in which it is mentioned in the New Testament** *(emphasis added).*[15]

As the action of leaven is destroyed by fire, the Apostate Church will ultimately be destroyed by fire.

The woman, who is the Apostate Church, is sitting on (that is, has the approval of) the Antichrist, an Islamic military leader.

> [3] *...And I saw a* **woman sitting on a scarlet beast** *which was full of names of blasphemy,* **having**

seven heads and ten horns. ⁴*The woman was arrayed in purple and scarlet, and adorned with gold and precious stones and pearls, having in her hand a golden cup full of abominations and the filthiness of her fornication.*

Revelation 17:3-4 (emphasis added)

She exists during the first half of the Tribulation. At this time, the Antichrist is only dominant in the Islamic world. The Roman (seventh) Kingdom is still reigning on the earth (Revelation 17:10). Paganism, goddess worship, and pantheism will unite with a false (apostate) Christianity in the Roman Empire. Christianity in the European Union will include a return to ancient pagan mystery religions. John describes the woman of Revelation:

⁵ *And on her forehead a name was written:*

MYSTERY BABYLON THE GREAT, THE MOTHER OF HARLOTS AND OF THE ABOMINATIONS OF THE EARTH.

Revelation 17:5

Harlotry in the Bible usually implies worship of a false god. Has the Church compromised with Islam and paganism? We know that Muslims will behead those who resist their doctrine (Revelation 6:4; 20:4). We see the Apostate Church, the woman, is also martyring the saints.

⁶ *I saw the woman, drunk with the blood of the saints and with the blood of the martyrs of Jesus. And when I saw her, I marveled with great amazement.*

Revelation 17:6

What a devastating, gut-wrenching scenario! The Church that Jesus loved, nourished and died for, has totally sold out to the evil one. It would be impossible to believe, if it had not been prophesied by so many credible witnesses (2 Thessalonians 2:3; 2 Timothy 3:1-5; Matthew 13:33).

Because Revelation 17 is a mystery and God does not want us to be confused, he sends an angel to explain to John what he is seeing. The angel says "...I will tell you the mystery of the woman..." (Revelation 17:7). The chart below shows what John saw and how the angel interpreted it.

REVELATION	
What John Saw	**The Angel's Interpretation**
She is "...the great harlot that sits on many waters..". (17:1)	"The waters which you saw, where the harlot sits, are peoples, multitudes, nations and tongues". (17:15)
[We see here a picture of a universal church engulfed in harlotry, a false Christianity.]	
What John Saw	**The Angel's Interpretation**
She was "...sitting on a scarlet beast...having seven heads..". (17:3)	"The seven heads are seven mountains on which the woman sits" (17:9)
[The seven mountains are seen by various authors to be the seven hills of Rome or seven continents or seven kingdoms against Israel.]	
What John Saw	**The Angel's Interpretation**
"...I saw a woman siting on a scarlet beast...having seven heads and ten horns", (17:3)	"There are also seven kings". (17:10)
[Egypt, Assyria, Babylon, Medo-Persia, Greece, Rome and Revived Rome]	
"And the woman whom you saw is..". (17:18)	"...that great city which reigns over the kings of the earth". (17:18)
[This is Rome the center of the Revived Roman Empire.]	

One might pose the question: Why not just address Mystery Babylon by her actual name, which is Rome? There are several possible explanations:

1. John is following a precedent set by Peter, who referred to Rome as Babylon in 1 Peter 5:13.

2. Mystery Babylon is a harlot. Harlotry in the Bible implies worship of false gods. Paganism began in Babylon, the cradle of civilization. "Mystery Babylon" denotes total capitulation of the once holy Church to the powers of darkness.

3. The Apostle John called the city, "Mystery Babylon" as a code word, instead of Rome. John encodes the name to avert possible retaliation from the Roman government (see page 66).

We notice in verse 12 that one of the first official acts of the ten kings, who begin their world domination mid-Tribulation, under the authority of the Antichrist, is to burn Rome. It is highly probable the Antichrist requires them to destroy Rome as an act of allegiance to him.

> [12] *The ten horns which you saw are ten kings who have received no kingdom as yet, but they receive authority for one hour as kings with the beast.*

> [16] *And the ten horns which you saw on the beast, these will hate the harlot, make her desolate and naked, eat her flesh and burn her with fire.*
>
> Revelation 17:12, 16

Such irony! This Apostate Church, which embraced the theology of the world, is ultimately destroyed by those with whom she compromised!

Some of the compromises the Apostate Church embraces, the "doctrines of demons" as it were, include the following:

1. There are many roads to God. Worship any god you want, any way you want. Goddess worship has been suppressed by a male-dominated society.

2. The Bible is a good book if it helps you. It is not the inspired word of God and is not infallible. *already*

3. Abortion is an individual decision between a woman, her doctor, and her god. *already*

4. Sexual preferences are inborn traits. God made people that way and approves of their lifestyle. *already* *(illegible) gone,*

5. God is finished with the Jews; the Church has replaced them. *not so*

6. Jesus was a good man and a prophet. He is not God; He did not die for our sins. *Islam already*

Beloved, if your Church teaches any of the above doctrines, RUN, DON'T WALK, to the nearest exit and never look back. "*There is a way that seems right to a man, but its end is the way of death*" (Proverbs 14:12). Many people who are left behind and read this book after the Rapture will recognize doctrines their Church embraced in this list. Thankfully, it is not too late for you. Search the Scriptures and repent. God still has a high call for your life.

For seven cataclysmic years the Jews will suffer indignation one last time.

You can still serve God. You can be their friend.

CHAPTER 12

GOD'S CHOSEN PEOPLE

In this book we identify the first 2,000 years of human history as the "Age of Conscience". The Jews, however, identify this period as the "Era of Desolation" or the "Age of Chaos". Adam had sinned; Abel had been murdered; and then mankind had fallen into idolatry. Ten generations had simultaneously drowned in the Deluge. Even after God raised up righteous Noah, men disobeyed God, failing to replenish and "fill the earth" (Genesis 9:1). They huddled instead on the plain of Shinar, following the orders of Nimrod and building the idolatrous Tower at Babel.

God's answer to this continual rebellion was to carve out

a people for Himself, people with whom He could covenant. Abraham was born in the Jewish year 1948. Because of his character and obedience to God, the "Age of the Law" began. Abraham not only left his nation (modern Iraq) and his relatives at God's command, but departed to "*the land that I will show you*" (Genesis 12:1). By packing up his family, not knowing where they would go, Abraham showed great courage and faith. He became the "Father" of both Jews and Christians (see Galatians 3:29). For the rest of his life, Abraham and his family dwelt in tents, never building himself a home for this purpose: When God told Him to move, he could pull up stakes and be immediately obedient. God promised Abraham:

> [3] *I will bless those who bless you,*
> *And I will curse him who curses you;*
> *And in you all the families of the earth shall be*
> *blessed".*

Genesis 12:3

This great truth of Genesis 12:3 is just as eternal and unequivocal as the Ten Commandments. Do you want to be blessed? Bless the Jews. Here is God's modus operandi in relation to the Jews:

- God blesses the Jews directly.

- God blesses the nations through the Jews.

- God judges the nations directly.

- God judges the Jews through the nations.

Abraham had two sons, Isaac, the father of the Jews, and Ishmael, the father of the Arabs. Today there are about 500 million Arabs, descendants of Ishmael. Yet there are only about 15 million Jews on planet earth. What accounts for the disparate number of progeny of the two sons of Abraham? This and this alone: Satan has dedicated himself throughout human history to destroying the Jews, God's Chosen People.

Satan's final attempt to destroy the Jews, in tandem with Antichrist, will occur during the Tribulation Period. Here is a summary of how Daniel describes that seven year period also called "Daniel's seventieth week".

> [27] *Then he (the Antichrist) shall confirm a covenant (a peace treaty) with many (probably Jews and Revived Roman Empire/Muslims) for one week (Daniel's 70th week);*
> *But in the middle of the week (3 ½ years later)*
> *He shall bring an end to (Temple) sacrifice and offering.*
> *And on the wing of abominations shall be one (image of the beast) who makes desolate,*
> *Even until the consummation (conclusion), which is determined (by the return of the Lord), is poured out on the desolate.*
>
> Daniel 9:27
> (words in parenthesis added by author)

Later in the Book of Daniel we learn the Tribulation will be "...*a time of trouble such as never was since there was a nation*" (Daniel 12:1). Jeremiah referred to it as the time of "*Jacob's trouble*" (Jeremiah 30:7).

SATAN'S PLAN TO DESTROY THE JEWS

But why is this time so dangerous for God's chosen people? The answer is startling and shocking. Satan and Antichrist will team up in an attempt to kill every single Jew on the planet who believes in the one true God. But why? Because Satan and Antichrist understand that if no Jews remain alive to cry out for their Messiah (Jesus) to return, He will never come.

Let us look at this truth in Hosea 5. In verse 14, God is like a "lion" to Ephraim (the ten northern tribes) and like a "young lion" to Judah (the two southern tribes). A lion totally pulverizes its prey; the ten northern tribes are thus called the "lost" tribes. They were totally decimated. A young lion leaves its prey in chunks; the two southern tribes remained intact but defeated by Nebuchadnezzar. Thus the Scripture was fulfilled:

> *14 For I will be like a lion to Ephraim, And like a young lion to the house of Judah. I, even I, will tear them and go away; I will take them away, and no one shall rescue.*
>
> Hosea 5:14

In the next verse we see the Messiah *"returns again to His place"*. (The only member of the Godhead to leave His place was Jesus.) Here we learn He will remain in His place until "they earnestly seek Him". In other words, Jesus' return to earth at the end of the Tribulation is predicated upon the Jews crying out to Him to come.

> *15 I will return again to My place*
> *Till they acknowledge their offense.*
> *Then they will seek My face;*
> *In their affliction they will earnestly seek Me".*
>
> Hosea 5:15

Their "offense" was not acknowledging Him as their Messiah.

In the next chapter we learn He will return "after two days (2,000 years)".

> *1 Come, and let us return to the Lord;*
> *For He has torn, but He will heal us;*
> *He has stricken, but He will bind us up.*
> *2 After two days He will revive us;*

On the third day He will raise us up,
That we may live in His sight.

Hosea 6:1,2

Jesus re-enforces the principle that the Jews must call to Him before He returns in the New Testament, in the gospel of Matthew.

> [37] *"O Jerusalem, Jerusalem, the one who kills the prophets and stones those who are sent to her! How often I wanted to gather your children together, as a hen gathers her chicks under her wings, but you were not willing!* [38] *See! Your house is left to you desolate;* [39] *for I say to you, you shall see Me no more till you say, 'Blessed is He who comes in the name of the Lord!'"*

Matthew 23:37-39

Mike Bickle explains further in his "Onething 2009 teaching Notes":

> *"Satan seeks to exploit Jesus' prophecy in Matthew 23:39 as a 'loophole' in God's end-time plan by seeking to keep the leaders of Israel from receiving Jesus as King.* **Satan wants to demonstrate that Jesus' prophetic word is false. Satan's strategy is to kill the entire Jewish race or to see that they are so offended at Jesus that they will never receive Him as their king.**
>
> *Jesus will not forcibly take the kingship over Israel but will wait until it is given to Him by those in positions of authority over the land. He prophesied that He would not come back to Jerusalem until the governmental leaders of Israel voluntarily asked Him to reign over them. Jesus "bound" Himself by this prophecy to only come back after Israel's leadership invite Him".* [16]

This sets up an exciting end-time drama, as Jesus returns from heaven on a white horse and presents Himself to the leaders of Israel probably on Yom Kippur (the Day of Atonement). He shows them His nail scars and promises:

> [10] *"And I will pour on the house of David and on the inhabitants of Jerusalem the Spirit of grace and supplication; then they will look on Me whom they pierced. Yes, they will mourn for Him as one mourns for his only son, and grieve for Him as one grieves for a firstborn.*
>
> Zechariah 12:10

The "type" for this future emotion-packed reunion is presented to us in the Book of Genesis, as Joseph is reunited with his family in Egypt:

> [14] *Then he fell on his brother Benjamin's neck and wept, and Benjamin wept on his neck.* [15]*Moreover he kissed all his brothers and wept over them, and after that his brothers talked with him.*
>
> [29] *So Joseph made ready his chariot and went up to Goshen to meet his father Israel; and he presented himself to him, and fell on his neck and wept on his neck a good while.*
>
> Genesis 45:14, 15; 46:29

The fulfillment of this dramatic reunion occurs in Zechariah 12:10. At this time all Israel will be "born again" in a single day, fulfilling a promise in Isaiah 66. (An intermediate fulfillment occurred on May 14, 1948 when the political nation of Israel was born. A final fulfillment occurs when the nation of Israel is "born from above" in one day.)

> [8] *Who has heard such a thing?*
> *Who has seen such things?*

Shall the earth be made to give birth in one day?
Or shall a nation be born at once?
For as soon as Zion was in labor,
She gave birth to her children.

Isaiah 66:8

The great Apostle Paul confirms this truth in the Book of Romans.

²⁶ *And so all Israel will be saved, as it is written:*

"The Deliverer will come out of Zion,
And He will turn away ungodliness from Jacob;
²⁷ *For this is My covenant with them,*
When I take away their sins".

Romans 11:26, 27

ENDTIME JEWS AND RIGHTEOUS GENTILES

The Lord gave Sister Jeanne Wilkerson, one of the most respected prophets in the 20th century, His desire for the End Time Church in relation to the Jews. It reads in part:

"...and the Church, the heart of the message that I'm going to give you and develop in you is going to be definitely drawn and concerned for the Jew again, sayeth the Lord of Hosts. I'm going to give you a love for them. They're going to sense and know that you are My disciples by the love that you will show toward them. It was them, it was through them and by them that you enlightened that you were brought into the kingdom of God. It was their message that brought the Light unto you who were Gentiles sayeth the Spirit of the Living God. Therefore you owe a debt to Israel. You owe a debt that only this generation will be able to

– 167 –

pay. And this generation is going to pay this debt in full, sayeth the Spirit of the Living God". [17]

This support from the true Church is essential, as the world descends into anti-Semitism. After we are Raptured, the righteous Gentiles will take our place. In a video address in September, 2013, Israeli Prime Minister Benjamin Netanyahu gave this onerous assessment:

"What was unfashionable is now becoming fashionable again. What is fashionable today is to say: 'Well, I don't hate Jews – I just don't think they should have a state' or, effectively, that their state is an illegitimate one that doesn't have a right to exist". [18]

This is the prevailing view in Iran. On February 5, 2012, Iranian strategist and colleague of Ayatolla Khamene, Alireza Forghani declared the following on the Iranian website "Alef". Iran has legal and religious reasons to destroy Israel and all Jews. Calling Jews "corrupting material" and "a cancerous tumor", Iran pledges itself to taking the lead in destroying them all.[19] (Recall that "Persia" changed its name to "Iran" in 1935. The name "Iran" is a transliteration of Hitler's favorite word "Aryan".)

Today the political leadership of Iran has two major goals. They want to improve economically and advance "scientifically" – code for acquiring nuclear bombs.

Iran is one of the four ancient enemies of Israel, first identified in Daniel 2. It is a "goat nation", and apparently will not go into the Millennial reign (Daniel 2:35). Inexplicably, approximately 15,000 Jews remain in Iran, and even hold one seat in the Iranian Parliament.

WORLD WAR II AS A TYPE OF END TIMES

King Solomon declared long ago that "there is nothing new under the sun" (Ecclesiastes 1:9). The Bible presents a series of "types" that foreshadow future fulfillments. Adolph Hitler was a "type" of the Antichrist. With this understanding in mind, we are going to look at the attack on Poland that began World War II. Poland was unique for several reasons:

1. The Jews in the ghetto in Warsaw, Poland were the only ones that rebelled against the Nazis.

2. Poland was the only nation receiving large amounts of funds from expatriated countrymen who had escaped to Great Britain. This illustrates the true mettle of this great people.

3. More Polish Jews died (about 3 million) than Jews from any other nation.

4. Most of the extermination camps were in Poland.

5. Many Polish religious clerics (mostly Catholic) died at the hands of the Nazis.

6. Hitler considered all Poles to be subhuman, and planned to use them as a servant class in the future Aryan society.

The following information illustrates how quickly events occurred, once the Nazis invaded Poland on September 1, 1939.

- October 1939: Jews could not leave the country and their bank accounts were frozen. Jews were denied any welfare benefits. Jews were drafted into forced labor teams.

- Saturday, October 28 – census of all Jews.

[Regarding Polish citizens also: all radios had to be surrendered. Furthermore, possession of a radio transmitter was punishable by death].

- November 1939 – All Jews age ten and over must wear a Star of Zion on their right sleeve. All Jewish shops must place a Star of Zion near the entrance.

- December 1939 – All Jewish schools were closed, and Jews were forbidden from entering Aryan hospitals. Jews could not practice law or run mortgage and loan institutions.

- January 1940 – Jewish synagogues and yeshivas were closed. Jewish males, ages 12 to 60, must register for forced labor.

- September 1940 – Trams were for Aryans only, except for cars marked "for Jews".

- October 1940 – All Jews in Warsaw must leave their homes for the Jewish district.

- November 1940 – The Jewish district was sealed with a brick fence for "sanitary reasons".

- July 1942 – All Jews in Warsaw not working for the Germans will be "evacuated". (code for exterminated).

We see from the timeline above how quickly Hitler and his evil henchmen executed their murderous plan. We know the reign of the Antichrist is 42 months (Revelation 13:5). Expect him to be equally evil and demonic.

The Lord has provided an escape plan for His Jews, an airlift into Petra in Jordan. It will occur midway through the Tribulation. However, there are prerequisites.

1. Jews must know the plan, explained in Matthew 24:15-20

2. They must already live in Israel ("Judea" in verse 16) in order to escape.

3. They must drop everything and run when the abomination of desolation (image of the beast) is set up, verses 17-20.

4. They will, in all probability, be airlifted from Ben Gurion airport to Petra. Revelation 12:6, 14

5. They will be the first group saved when Jesus returns at the end of the Tribulation in Isaiah 63:1-6

There is no guarantee that American Jews will be safe. History tells us that the Jews were great industrialists, scientists and physicians in Germany before Hitler ascended to power. Yet they were all targeted by Hitler. Americans who are "left behind" must be prepared to hide and protect the Jews in the Western Hemisphere, if necessary.

Let us return to the subject of World War II as the best type of this future evil. It is important to remember that one of the "perks" enjoyed by the SS was they were allowed to keep the wealth they confiscated from the Jews. In Daniel 11 we learn Antichrist will *"divide the land for gain"* (verse 39). In verse 43 we learn *"He shall have power over the treasures of gold and silver..."*

Expect the Antichrist's followers to enrich themselves at the expense of the Jews. Revelation 18 clearly describes merchants as the "great" men of the earth during that time. Many of those who take the mark of the beast will be the "beautiful people", ensconced in yachts and palatial homes. Wealth continues to attract evil men, until it all goes up in smoke at the end of the Tribulation.

> ¹⁸ *and cried out when they saw the smoke of her burning, saying, 'What is like this great city?'*
> ¹⁹ *They threw dust on their heads and cried out, weeping and wailing, and saying, 'Alas, alas, that great city, in which all who had ships on the sea became rich by her wealth! For in one hour she is made desolate.'*
>
> Revelation 18:18,19

The purpose of this chapter is to tug at your heart strings, so you will love and publicly stand with the Jews. However, even if one is without natural affection, it is still folly to stand against the Jews. Why? God is on their side.

It will seem, during the Great Tribulation, that all hope is lost for the Jews. It will be a time of unparalleled suffering. Zechariah 13:8 tells us that two thirds of the Jews in the land shall die. The future "death camps" will be located primarily in the Middle East. Anguish continues until Jesus returns. Mike Bickle explains it like this:

> *"Jesus will march through these nations killing His enemies and liberating Jewish prisoners in death camps and healing the infirm (blind, lame, etc.; Isaiah 35:4-6; 61:1,2; 42:6-7, 16; Micah 4:6). Jesus will function as the "greater Moses". An essential part of the Second Coming procession involves Jesus marching from Egypt through Assyria back to*

Israel liberating Jews in death camps. Jews being in prison camps in the End-Times is one of the most prominent features in Second Coming passages (in the OT prophets). This truth is usually dismissed and ignored".[20]

However, ignoring evil is a foolish and dangerous position. Rather, we must prepare for future events that are tragic and inevitable. Amazingly, the evil Adolph Hitler understood it.

TO SEE THE FUTURE YOU MUST LOOK BACKWARDS

1. The war for world domination will be fought entirely between us and the Jews. All else is facade and illusion. **Adolf Hitler**

2. Those who do not learn from history are doomed to repeat it. **Edmund Burke**

3. The Sages tell us to study history carefully. For what happened to our forebears is bound to happen again to us. **The Ramban**

We close this chapter by noting common factors between World War II and World War III (the Armageddon scenario).

1. Church in Apostasy - "German Christians" stood with Hitler; Harlot Church of Revelation 17:6

2. Leader Demonic - A. Hitler; Antichrist - Daniel 11:37, 38

3. (Attempted) Assassination of Hitler - Valkyrie and other plots during World War II; Antichrist really dies - Zechariah 11:17, Revelation 13:12, 14

4. Short reign of Terror - Hitler 1939 - 1945; Antichrist 42 months - Revelation 13:5

5. Major goal is to kill all Jews - Hitler's "Final Solution"; Antichrist's plan to thwart the return of the LORD - Matthew 23:39

6. Nuclear Weapons in play - Used to end WW II; WW III will be a nuclear war (implied) - Zechariah 14:12 & Ezekiel 29:11-13

CHAPTER 13

THE UNHOLY TRINITY

The unholy trinity, which joins together during the seven year Tribulation Period, has as its purpose to overthrow God, seize Jerusalem and rule the world. As God is love (I John 4:7-8), this evil trio is hatred incarnate. Although they work together, Satan, Antichrist and the false prophet are motivated by a selfish desire for the advancement of their own personal gain. Their cooperation with each other is motivated only out of love of self and hatred for humanity. Most Bible scholars have traditionally held that the "evil trinity" will include Satan, Antichrist and the false prophet.

SATAN (IMITATOR OF OUR HEAVENLY FATHER)

Also called the dragon, the deceiver and the accuser of the brethren, Satan fell long before God created Adam (Ezekiel 28:13–17). By deceiving Eve in the Garden of Eden, he persuaded our first parents to turn over their authority and dominion of planet earth. (Thankfully, Jesus bought back our right to dominion with His death on the cross. Through faith, we take back our authority.) Satan and his hordes do not want men to receive the free gift of salvation through the Blood of Jesus. They have dedicated themselves, throughout human history, to destroying men's souls. Satan is very familiar with Biblical prophecy, and knows his end is near. He is enraged, because he will soon be bound in hell (Revelation 20:2). In an effort to take as many souls as possible with him, he will make a deal with Antichrist to conquer and deceive the world. Many scholars believe Satan will offer Antichrist the same deal he tried to persuade Jesus to take.

> [5] Then the devil, taking Him up on a high mountain, showed Him all the kingdoms of the world in a moment of time. [6] And the devil said to Him, **"All this authority I will give You,** and their glory; for this has been delivered to me, and I give it to whomever I wish. [7] Therefore, **if You will worship before me,** all will be Yours".
>
> Luke 4:5–7 (emphasis added)

Jesus, of course, **declined** the evil offer. **Antichrist will accept it**.

> [2]... The dragon gave him (Antichrist) his power, his throne and great authority.
>
> Revelation 13:2
> (parenthesis are author's opinion)

During the first half of the Tribulation Period, Satan

will destroy souls primarily through three
paganism, Islam and the Apostate Church.

1. Paganism — This ancient polytheistic worship has
   been practiced since antiquity. The sun, moon
   and planets were worshiped by primitive men.
   Today the "green" movement again worships
   nature and elevates animals to the status of
   human beings. !! Abortion

Ancient pagan mother-son worship was founded in the
era of Nimrod (Genesis 11:4). A widely popular blasphemous
novel trumpets worship of female deities. The following
false deities, the stuff of mythology for generations, is
now being reconstructed in post Christian Europe as true
"deities", deserving of worship. See chart below of mother/
son worship.

MOTHER-SON WORSHIP

COUNTRY	MOTHER	SON
Babylon	Semiramis	Tammuz
Egypt	Isis	Osiris
Assyria	Ishtar	Bacchus
India	Isi	Iswara
Greece	Aphrodite	Eros
Rome	Venus	Cupid

2. Islam — It is the avowed purpose of radical
   fundamentalist (Shiite, Sunnis and Wahabi) Islam
   to conquer the world for Allah. Mohammad's
   command as he lay dying was, "Fight until all
   declare, there is no god but Allah, and Mohammad
   is his prophet". Militaristic Muslims believe Sharia

law must rule the globe. Many moderate Muslims, probably a statistical majority, do not agree with Sharia law. In western countries, we see brave Muslim women speaking out against it.

Sharia law includes stonings, flagellations, hand amputation for stealing, no usury, limitations on women (need men's permission to be educated, vote, marry, drive) and the right for men to have up to four wives.

An especially egregious aspect of Sharia law is "honor killings". If a Muslim pledges a female relative to another Muslim in marriage, the female relative must comply, even if the proposed groom already has several wives. If she refuses the arrangement, her male family member may brutally murder her, a so-called "honor killing".

Those who do not agree with militant Islam are executed by beheading. As we hear of more and more beheadings in the Middle East, our society is becoming numbed by its horror. As the executioner severs the head with his sword, he cries out, "Allahu akbar". "Allahu akbar" translates as "Allah is greater (or greatest)".

It's a comparison between Allah and Jehovah. After the Rapture it shall appear, for a season, that Islam is indeed the defeater of Christianity.

3. The Apostate Church—After the Rapture of the Bride of Christ, the Church that remains will fall into total apostasy, according to the Apostle Paul.

> *[1] Now the Spirit expressly says that in latter times some will depart from the faith, giving heed to deceiving spirits and doctrines of demons,*
> I Timothy 4:1

[3] Let no one deceive you by any means; for that Day

*(the Day of the Lord, the wrath of Jehovah) will
not come unless the falling away comes first, and
the man of sin is revealed, the son of perdition
(mid-Tribulation).*

2 Thessalonians 2:3
(parenthesis author's interpretation)

It is highly likely that the Apostate Church will be controlled by a high ranking prelate who operates out of Rome, Italy (see Chapter 11). The Church has the tacit approval of the European Union to give the population "*...a form of godliness, but denying its power"* , 2 Timothy 3:5. The European rulers will condescend to give the masses of people "religion" (the "opiate of the people" as Karl Marx called it). In Europe today most countries have a state Church, funded by the government. True Christians in Europe (including Fundamentalists, Pentecostals and Evangelicals) are branded as "cults" and outlawed in some countries already.

The era of the Apostate Church will be only three and a half years. Mid-Tribulation, when Antichrist seizes power from the European Union, he requires the ten kings to destroy the Apostate Church (Revelation 17:16). The kings do this to prove their loyalty, the price required to be co-rulers with Antichrist of the one world kingdom (Revelation 17:12-13).

The role of winning the lost returns to the Jews during the Tribulation. Specifically, we see Elijah and the other prophet raise up 144,000 Jewish evangelists in Revelation 7.

Mid-Tribulation the Apostate Church will be burned, Antichrist worship will emerge, and everyone will be required to join. Dear reader, notice that all other religions (apostate Christianity, Islam and paganism) have one thing in common. Namely, anyone seduced by them can escape judgment by coming to Jesus.

That is why the religion that replaces them is a thousand times more evil. Once a person accepts this religion, Antichrist worship, his soul is forever lost.

> [9] *Then a third angel followed them, saying with a loud voice, "If anyone worships the beast and his image, and receives his mark on his forehead or on his hand,* [10] *he himself shall also drink of the wine of the wrath of God, which is poured out full strength into the cup of His indignation. He shall be tormented with fire and brimstone in the presence of the holy angels and in the presence of the Lamb.* [11] *And the smoke of their torment ascends forever and ever; and they have no rest day or night, who worship the beast and his image, and whoever receives the mark of his name"*.
>
> Revelation 14:9-11 (emphasis added)

ANTICHRIST
(IMITATOR OF OUR LORD JESUS)

Antichrist, an Islamic political leader who comes from Syria, has spent three and a half years solidifying his Islamic base (see page 85). Now he seizes Jerusalem (Daniel 11:41) and conquers Egypt, Libya and Ethiopia (Daniel 11:42-43). Before he can totally destroy the Jews, he is distracted by rebellion in the east and the north, possibly China and Russia (Daniel 11:44).

At some point before he seized Jerusalem, an attempt had been made on his life, possibly a bullet through his right eye. (Keep in mind that prophets could only use words in their vocabulary: eagles for airplanes, swords for guns, chariots for tanks, etc.).

> *17Woe to the worthless shepherd, Who leaves the flock! **A sword shall be against his arm And against his right eye;** His arm shall completely wither, And his right eye shall be totally blinded.*
>
> Zechariah 11:17 (emphasis added)

His life is saved, by evil supernatural power. Could it be that the false prophet, head of the Apostate Church, saved his life? When Antichrist's breath returned could that be the moment he became indwelt by the evil demonic prince Apollyon (see Chapter 10)? Where Scripture is silent, we can only speculate.

> *3And I saw one of his heads as if it had been mortally wounded, **and his deadly wound was healed.** And all the world marveled and followed the beast.*
>
> Revelation 13:3 (emphasis added)

> *4...and they worshiped the beast saying, "Who is like the beast? Who is able to make war with him?"*
>
> Revelation 13:4

> *7It was granted to him to make war with the saints and to overcome them. And authority was given him over every tribe, tongue, and nation. 8All who dwell on the earth will worship him, whose names have not been written in the Book of Life of the Lamb slain from the foundation of the world.*
>
> Revelation 13:7-8

It is clear from the Scriptures that Antichrist's remarkable recovery has given him great stature in the eyes of the world. His influence will be felt worldwide. He will be a man of great wealth (Daniel 8:24 & 11:36). As Hitler appropriated the wealth and property of the Jews in World War II, Antichrist and his cohorts will confiscate the wealth of those who resist his control. One of Antichrist's titles will be "King of Babylon" (Isaiah 14:4). Babylon is in modern Iraq. Notice that great wealth and commerce flow through Iraq throughout the Tribulation Period.

> [3] *...and the merchants of the earth have become rich through the abundance of her luxury.*
> Revelation 18:3

> [12] *merchandise of gold and silver, precious stones and pearls, fine linen and purple, silk and scarlet, every kind of citron wood, every kind of object of ivory, every kind of object of most precious wood, bronze, iron, and marble;* [13] *and cinnamon and incense, fragrant oil and frankincense, wine and oil, fine flour and wheat, cattle and sheep, horses and chariots, **and bodies and souls of men**.*
> Revelation 18:12-13 (emphasis added)

THE FALSE PROPHET
(IMITATOR OF THE HOLY SPIRIT)

There are many types of the false prophet in history. The Jewish high priest, Menelaus, aided the evil Antiochus Epiphanes in the era of the Maccabeans.

The evil German bishop, Ludwig Muller, sold his soul for Hitler. As the official Reich bishop he encouraged the hapless German Christians to follow Adolph Hitler.

But the clearest picture of the false prophet is seen in Baalam, the Old Testament prophet who was stopped by God from cursing the Jews (Numbers: 22 and 23). But Baalam succeeded in destroying the Jews; he taught them to commit sexual immorality.

Four characteristics of the false prophet we can ascertain from the Baalam model are:

1. He once was a true prophet of God (Numbers 24:2).

2. He despises the Jews and true believers. (Jude 11)

3. He gives the Apostate Church permission to preach sexual immorality as not deviant, but ordained of God (Revelation 2:14).

4. He is motivated by greed (2 Peter 2:15).

Many scholars believe the false prophet will be the leader of the Apostate Church. When he sees the Church will be burned mid-Tribulation, he ingratiates himself with Antichrist in an effort to hold on to power. He is granted the power to perform lying signs and wonders (Revelation 13:13).

The false prophet deceives the masses by the great signs he does, such as causing fire to fall from heaven to earth (Revelation 13:13). It's interesting to note that the Antichrist controls him. The false prophet is permitted to work signs only when he is in the presence of the beast (Revelation 13:14; 19:20).

The chart on the adjoining two pages illustrates some aspects of the false prophet's role, which we can know for certain.

The end game for the false prophet and the Antichrist is the lake of fire. Many will follow them there. Dear reader, that punishment is eternal. We urge you now, if you are unsure of the final destination of your own soul, not to take any chances. Turn to page 207 of this book and bowing your knee to Jesus, ask Him to be the Lord of your life, as well as your Savior.

Characteristics of The False Prophet	Reference in the Book of Revelation
1. The world sees him as a "man of God", a spiritual leader.	"...he had two horns like a lamb..". (13:11)
2. His power is from Satan.	"...and spoke like a dragon". (13:11)
3. He performs deceiving signs and wonders.	"And he deceives those who dwell on the earth by the signs he was granted to do in the sight of the beast..". (13:14)
4. His authority is limited. He can only operate in the presence of Antichrist.	"...those signs which he was granted to do in the sight of the beast". (13:14)
5. He orders men (probably scientists) to create an image to the beast.	"...telling those who dwell on the earth to make an image to the beast..". (13:14)

Characteristics of The False Prophet continued	Reference in the Book of Revelation continued
6. He uses his evil power to make the image breathe.	"He was granted power to give breath to the image..". (13:15)
7. He orders death for those who do not worship the image.	"...and cause as many as would not worship the image of the beast to be killed. (13:15)
8. His orders extend to all of humanity, worldwide.	"He causes all, both small and great, rich and poor, free and slave..". (13:16)
9. He "seals mankind, and all who are sealed are eternally lost. (Contrast that with God's prophet, who sealed 144,000 for Jesus at the beginning of the Tribulation.)	"...to receive a mark on their right hand or their foreheads". (13:16) [See Revelation 7:37]
10. He forbids unsealed people from buying food, clothing and homes, holding jobs, sending their children to school or participating in society on any level.	"...no one may buy or sell except one who has the mark or the number of his name". (13:17)

THE IMAGE OF THE BEAST

What or who is the image of the beast? Many theories have been forwarded. Let us begin with what the Word of God records:

1. The image is in some way representative of the anti-christ. Those who worship it will be honoring the Antichrist (Revelation 14:9).

2. The image, also called "the abomination of desolation", will reside in the Temple Holy Place (Daniel 9:27 and Matthew 24:15).

3. The image is man-made, and it's creation is ordered by the false prophet (Revelation 13:14).

4. Presumably the image is never sent to hell or the lake of fire. The Bible describes the judgment of Satan (Revelation 20:2-3), the Antichrist (Revelation 19:20) and the false prophet (Revelation 19:20). Possibly the image of the beast starves to death. Being man-made, it ceases to be (Zechariah 11:8, 9).

Why would Antichrist desire an image to be created?

Many scholars believe evil supernatural forces will raise Antichrist up, after he receives a deadly head wound as we have already explained (Zechariah 11:17, Revelation 13:3, 12, 14). He will desire to create a kingdom that will last a 1,000 years to simulate the 1,000 year Millennial Reign of Jesus. Could this deadly wound cause Antichrist to contemplate his own mortality? Could he desire an heir, but one in his image only, an image that could speak and be worshiped (Revelation 13:15)? A natural child, born of a wife, would never be acceptable. The Antichrist considers women to be inferior beings (Daniel 11:37).

The false prophet comes to him with a suggestion.

"Science has progressed, and we could use their technology. **You could be cloned!**"

The false prophet orders the image to be created:

> [14] *And he (the false prophet) deceives those who dwell on the earth...**telling those who dwell on the earth to make an image to the beast** who was wounded by the sword and lived.*
>
> Revelation 13:14 (emphasis added)

The Word of God goes on to say:

> [15] *He was granted power to give breath to the image of the beast,*
>
> Revelation 13:15

In the New King James the word "power" is italicized because it was added at the privilege of the translator. By deleting it, we get a better understanding of this passage.

> [15] *He (the false prophet) was granted to give breath to the image of the beast,*
>
> Revelation 13:15
> (parenthesis author's interpretation)

This could be interpreted to mean this: As the "spiritual leader" of the entire world, (Revelation 13:11) the false prophet determines it is in the interest of the human family to have a successor to Antichrist. Antichrist is thought to be a god. Therefore, while human cloning is reprehensible to some people, consider the greater good, a guaranteed line of succession. As a spiritual guru, the false prophet has the "moral authority" to make this judgment.

In light of this possible interpretation of Revelation 13 we might also better understand a passage in 2 Thessalonians 2. This passage is addressed to those who reject the love of the truth (Jesus), during the Tribulation.

> *[11] And for this reason God will send them strong*
> *delusion, that they should believe the lie,*
>
> 2 Thessalonians 2:11

Scholars have asked the question, "What is the 'lie'?" Could the lie be this: **Antichrist is divine, and so is his image** (clone). Now the world could hardly be convinced to worship a hologram, robot, or computer that speaks. But if an infant were to speak, that would be remarkable.

As Dolly, the first cloned sheep grew to maturity at an accelerated rate, **possibly this clone of Antichrist will speak while still an infant** (Revelation 13:15).

According to Muslim legend, the Mahdi (awaited one), we know as Antichrist, was fully grown by the age of six and could speak from the womb. (In Muslim tradition he was born in the 9th century and will reappear at the end of days.) To see Antichrist's image, or cloned child, speaking as an infant, would help to confirm in the eyes of many people that they were indeed in the presence of a superior being. To those bent on getting rich by following the Antichrist anyway, worshiping such a baby would be easy to do.

Let us revisit Revelation 13:15 in the King James Version.

> *[15] And he had power to give **life** unto the image of*
> *the beast, that the image of **the beast should**
> ...**speak**...*
>
> Revelation 13:15 (KJV emphasis added)

In Revelation 13:15 <u>Strong's Concordance</u> defines "life" as #4151, "pneuma", which means breath, or a current of air. **It is the only time in the New Testament that this word is used for life.** Most references to the word "life" in the New Testament use the Greek word "zoe", which means life.   Eternal life is always referenced as eternal "zoe".

To understand "pneuma", from which we get our word pneumonia (infection in the lungs), we will use a medical analogy. A person may be clinically dead but still breathing via a respirator in an intensive care unit. A current of air is blowing in and out of the lungs and the heart continues to beat. In some cases the "zoe" life comes back and the person opens his eyes and returns to normal.

Sometimes these people say that they were "out of their bodies" for a period of time, in heaven or in hell.

What we can glean from the original Greek text is this: The image of the beast is given the ability to function as a **breathing entity**. The word for "image" is the Greek word "eikon" (Strong's Concordance #1504) which means likeness.   The English word "icon" is a transliteration of eikon.   We know that Jesus is the "eikon" of God (2 Corinthians 4:4).

Could it be that the beast (Antichrist) in his evil desire to imitate God allows the scientific community to develop his clone, desiring an "eikon" of himself? The image of the beast will be a "breathing likeness" of the beast according to the Greek text.

In R. Edwin Sherman's book, Bible Code Bombshell, he discusses a cluster of hidden messages in Ezekiel 37. The thrust of these codes is clearly eschatological. An especially intriguing message, which could reference a cloned image of the beast reads like this: **"The newborn one is a father with no yesterday. His name will melt as bait"**.[21]

This passage could reference a male child with no natural heritage. If this is the image of the beast, it is indeed bait. Those who worship it will perish. "His name will melt.." could imply that not being human, it ceases to exist after the Tribulation.

As previously mentioned, the Bible does not mention a judgment for the image of the beast. According to the Rabbi Moshe Botschko, "In my opinion, a creature born through genetic duplication is not considered human—it is clear beyond all doubt that the life form created in some scientific institution will be an animal that walks on two feet, no more". [22]

The specter of such a humanoid baby set in the Temple Holy Place is daunting. God had no part in this creation. Will men come and worship this unholy thing, bringing it gifts? It is too horrible to contemplate.

As we close this extremely speculative section of the text, we acknowledge that we **do not know** what or who the image of the beast will be.

Here are the facts we do know to be true:

1. The original "abomination of desolation" was placed above the altar by Antiochus Epiphanes. It was a statue of Zeus with a face carved to look exactly like Antiochus Epiphanes.

2. Jesus is the express image of the Father.

3. Jesus affirmed an end time "abomination of desolation" would stand in the Holy Place (Mark 13:14). This could be the image of the beast.

4. Jewish folklore has always included a belief that a holy man (rabbi to them) would have the power to create a humanoid without the help of God. Such a being is called a "golem". Mary Shelley's best selling book from the nineteenth century, Frankenstein, is based on the Jewish belief that man could create life.

5. Since man was created in the image of God, he actually has extraordinary abilities. God Himself observed that man could do anything he attempted:

"...nothing that they (mankind) propose to do will be withheld from them" (Genesis 11:6) .

6. Whatever the image of the beast is, mankind will desire to worship it. God actually sends angels to be seen by men, warning them not to worship it (Revelation 14:9), because worshiping the image of the beast causes one to be eternally lost. The primary thrust of this section of the text is not to identify the image of the beast. It is to warn the reader, alive during the Tribulation Period, that worshiping the image of the beast will be a real temptation. In order to be found worthy to spend eternity with Jesus, you must be prepared to resist worshiping this unholy thing, whatever it is, and whatever power it displays.

666: THE NUMBER OF MANKIND

I began this chapter by declaring the traditional definition for the unholy trinity: Satan, Antichrist and the False Prophet. I will now present the reader with a second view of the unholy trinity. A view that would help explain the meaning of "666".

Revelation 13 introduces three persons: the Antichrist, the False Prophet and the Image of the Beast. This chapter concludes with this enigmatic verse:

> [18] *Here is wisdom. Let him who has understanding calculate the number of the beast, for* **it is the number of a man:** *His number is 666 .*
> Revelation 13:18 (emphasis added)

Although some older manuscripts contain the numbers "606", today we see it translated 666. Could these numbers represent three human beings? This is conjecture on my part , the following is only an interesting possibility.

THE UNHOLY TRINITY

father	**-**	**antichrist**
son	**-**	**image of the beast**
unholy spirit	**-**	**false prophet**

Several scriptures indicate that this interpretation is accurate. The Antichrist (the Bible rarely calls him the Antichrist) does not try to imitate Jesus, he tries to imitate the Father.

> [3] ...the man of sin is revealed, the son of perdition, [4]who opposes and exalts himself above all that is called God or that is worshiped, so that **he sits as God in the temple of God, showing himself that he is God.**
>
> 2 Thessalonians 2:3-4 (emphasis added)

"God" in this passage is #2316 in Strong's Concordance. The definition is "Theos, the supreme Divinity". In fact, usually when "Theos" is used in the New Testament it refers to the First Person of the Trinity.

And so, by declaring himself to be Theos, possibly Antichrist is declaring himself to be God Almighty, the first person of the Trinity.

The second person of the unholy trinity is the image of the beast. Remembering the Strong's Concordance #1504 shows the meaning of image as "eikon". Jesus is referred to as the "eikon" of the Father many times in the New Testament (1 Corinthians 11:7; 2 Corinthians 4:4; Colossians 1:15; Hebrews 1:3).

Could it be that the words, "eikon (image) of the beast"

were put in the Scripture by the Holy Spirit to give us a clue? Jesus is the express image of the Father. Let us also consider the words of Jesus Himself when He said, "...He who has seen Me has seen the Father;" (John 14:9). As a cloned human being, the image of the beast is the express image of the Antichrist.

King David prophesied that man would one day sever all relationships with the Godhead.

> *¹ Why do the nations rage, And the people plot a vain thing?*
> *² The kings of the earth set themselves, and the rulers take counsel together, Against the Lord, and against His Anointed, saying,*
> *³ **"Let us break Their bonds in pieces And cast away Their cords from us".***
>
> Psalm 2:1-3 (emphasis added)

According to Rashi, the great Jewish rabbi of the 11th century, the fulfillment of this verse immediately precedes the coming of Messiah. Christian sources agree with that interpretation.

It's a chilling fact that a totally human trinity is already worshiped by some in the Arab world. A controversial subset of Shia Muslims, the Nusaryis, worship a group of deceased human beings. The objects of their worship are Ali, Mohammad and Salman.

It could be that this trio of dead human beings worshiped as gods, foreshadow a future world religion. This new religion is represented by the number 666. This religion worships Antichrist, the image of the beast and the false prophet, three human entities. This totally human trinity will only endure for three and a half years.

When Adolph Hitler realized in 1944, that he would

lose World War II he ordered Germany and all occupied territories destroyed.

Thankfully, most of his generals ignored his orders.

Will Antichrist order the annihilation of planet earth? The Bible says if Jesus were not to shorten the days, all humanity would be destroyed (Matthew 24:22).

But Jesus will return, at precisely the correct moment in time. When the Father tells Him to, Jesus will leave His seat at the Father's right hand.

> [5] *The Lord is at Your right hand;*
>   *He shall execute kings in the day of His wrath.*
> [6] *He shall judge among the nations,*
>   *He shall fill the places with dead bodies,*
>   *He shall execute the heads of many countries.*
>   Psalm 110:5-6

Lightning will flash through the sky—lightning that begins in the east and then continues on progressing through the heavens until it reaches the west.

Men will tremble and shake with fear. Many suffer heart attacks. Women scream. The earth shakes convulsively. Nuclear bombs explode, dissolving human flesh and eyes. Hail stones the size of basketballs pelt the earth. Then a noise, an ear-splitting noise in the sky. All eyes turn toward heaven...

CHAPTER 14

MASHIACH BEN DAVID

essiah, son of David, will come out of the sky, riding a white horse, to punish the ungodly and save mankind from extinction (Matthew 24:22,30). The ancient Jewish prophet, Enoch, described His coming about 5,000 years ago. (Enoch was the great, great, great, great grandson of Adam, and the first human being to be Raptured.) Jude rerecords his ancient words in the New Testament.

> [14] *Now Enoch , the seventh from Adam, prophesied about these men also, saying, "Behold, the Lord comes with ten thousands of His saints,* [15] ***to execute judgment on all, to convict all who***

are ungodly among them of all their ungodly deeds which they have committed in an ungodly way, and of all the harsh things which ungodly sinners have spoken against Him".

Jude 14-15 (emphasis added)

The basic belief of Orthodox Jewry was framed by Maimonides in the 12th century A.D. *"I believe with complete faith in the coming of Messiah: and even though He tarry, I will wait for Him every coming day".*

The poignancy of Messiah's coming, the premier event in all of human history, cannot be overstated. The Jews have been hated and abused throughout history. Moses himself had prophesied this would happen (Deuteronomy 28:33). When all reason for hope is gone, death and destruction are everywhere, Messiah appears out of nowhere to save the Day! The coming of Messiah in victory at the end of the age has been taught since the beginning of time (Genesis 3:15). Consider for a moment, these faith-filled words of Job who may have been a contemporary of Abraham.

²⁵ **For I know that my Redeemer lives,**
  And He shall stand at last on the earth;
  ²⁶ *And after my skin is destroyed, this I know,*
  *That **in my flesh** I shall see God,*

Job 19:25-26 (emphasis added)

It is obvious from this passage that Job understood (probably handed down through the oral tradition) that he would one day have a glorified body. Job will receive that glorified body at the Rapture. A glorified body is a flesh and bone body, like Jesus has.

³⁹ *Behold My hands and My feet, that it is I Myself. Handle Me and see, for a spirit does not have flesh and bones as you see I have.*

Luke 24:39

[Notice we will still eat and drink when we have glorified "flesh and bone" bodies. Matthew 26:29, Luke 24:43 and John 21:15]

Paul declared that ultimately, our bodies would be redeemed.

> *²² For we know that the whole creation groans and labors with birth pangs together until now. ²³ Not only that, but we also who have the first fruits of the Spirit, even we ourselves groan within ourselves, **eagerly waiting for the adoption, the redemption of our body.***
>
> Romans 8:22–23 (emphasis added)

John confirms that glorious promise.

> *²Beloved, now we are children of God; and it has not yet been revealed what we shall be, but we know that when He is revealed, **we shall be like Him,** for we shall see Him as He is.*
>
> 1 John 3:2 (emphasis added)

The redemption of the Church and the Old Testament saints comes seven years before the redemption of the Jews. Oh, that glorious and soon-coming day! When our mortal bodies "put on" immortality, we will forever stand with Jesus as the "end time saints". We will not taste death. Dear reader, to reject this awesome testimony is to say: I would rather live in hell on earth for seven years than depart in victory and be transformed into His image.

WE WILL NOT TASTE DEATH

Listen to the great apostle, Paul.

> *²² If anyone does not love the Lord Jesus Christ, let him be accursed. O Lord, come!*
>
> 1 Corinthians 16:22

God showed the pagan king, Nebuchadnezzar, in a dream, the world powers that would reign during the "times of the Gentiles". Daniel, the greatly beloved prophet of God, was given the interpretation of this dream. Notice that the last world power to reign is the ten kings (ten toes).

The ten kings, and Antichrist their leader, are not destroyed by human beings. No, dear reader, **the Church will not overcome the evil one.** The privilege of defeating the evil world system is clearly delineated in Daniel 2:45.

> *[34] You watched **while a stone was cut out without hands,** which struck the image on its feet of iron and clay, and broke them in pieces. [35] "Then the iron, the clay, the bronze, the silver, and the gold were crushed together, and became like chaff from the summer threshing floors; the wind carried them away so that no trace of them was found. And the stone that struck the image became a great mountain and filled the whole earth".*
> Daniel 2:34, 35 (emphasis added)

And so we ask the question, who is the stone that destroys the evil world system? Jesus Himself is the stone.

> *[17] Then he looked at them and said, "What then is this that is written:*
>
> *'The stone which the builders rejected*
> *Has become the chief cornerstone?'*
>
> *[18] Whoever falls on that stone will be broken; but on whomever it falls, it will grind him to powder".*
> Luke 20:17-18 (emphasis added)

We recall that Satan ruled the world during the seven kingdoms of this age (Egypt, Assyria, Babylon, Medo-Persia, Greece, Rome and Revived Rome). Seven is the number of completion (seven days in a week, seven notes in a scale, seven thousand years in human history). After seven kingdoms have been completed, the Antichrist takes over mid-Tribulation, at the beginning of the Day of the Lord. The Antichrist kingdom is the eighth kingdom (Revelation 17:11). Eight is the number of "new beginnings". The Antichrist thinks he is setting up a 1,000 year reign.

Notice in the chart on the next two pages the events of this 3 $^1/_2$ year era are well chronicled, in both the Old and New Testaments on. **It is Jesus, and He alone, that defeats the Antichrist and the world system.**

	Old Testament	New Testament
Antichrist Seizes Jerusalem	"...the people of the prince who is to come shall destroy the city and the sanctuary..". Daniel 9:26	"And their dead bodies will lie in the street of the reat city which spiritually is called Sodom and Egypt, where also Our Lord was crucified. Revelation 11:8
Antichrist Declares He Is God	"...He shall exalt and magnify himself above every god..". Daniel 11:36	"...he sits as God in the temple of God showing himself that he is God". 2 Thessalonians 2:4
Michael Helps Out	"At that time Michael shall stand up, the great prince who stands watch over the sons of your people..". Daniel 12:1	"And war broke out in heaven; Michael and his angels fought with the dragon..". Revelation 12:7
Jehovah Gives Jesus Dominion	"...One like the Son of Man...to Him was given dominion and glory and a kingdom..". Daniel 7:13-14	"...The kingdoms of this world have become the kingdoms of our Lord And His Christ, and He shall reign forever and ever.'" Revelation 11:15

	Old Testament	New Testament
Jesus Puts In The Sickle	"Put in the sickle, for the harvest is ripe. Come, go down..". Joel 3:13	"...on the cloud sat One like the Son of Man...and in HIs hands a sharp sickle". Revelation 14:14
Jesus Treads The Winepress	"I have trodden the winepress alone..". Isaiah 63:3	"He Himself treads the winepress of the fierceness and wrath of Almighty God". Revelation 19:15b
Jesus' Garments Are Bloody	"Their blood is sprinkled upon My garments... Isaiah 63:3	"He was clothed with a robe dipped in blood..". Revelation 19:13
Jesus Acts Alone	"I looked, but there was no one to help... and My own fury, it sustained me". Isaiah 63:5	"...in righteousness He judges and makes war..". Revelation 19:11
Jesus Is Lord	"And the Lord shall be King over all the earth". Zechariah 14:9	"and on His thigh a name written: KING OF KINGS AND LORD OF LORDS". Revelation 19:16

We recall that it was Adam, the first man, who fell into sin. God promised Adam and Eve that He would send His holy seed to redeem humanity (Genesis 3:15). For 4,000 years, Satan has been trying to destroy the Jews and abort God's plan. Satan knew that if he were successful in annihilating the Jews, Messiah would never come. Repeated agents of Satan who have attempted to destroy the Jews include: Egyptians, Amalekites, Nebuchadnezzar, Haman, Antiochus Epiphanes, the Romans, the crusaders, the Spanish Inquisition, the Russian pogroms, the Third Reich, the Islamic terrorists and, very soon, the Antichrist.

In some Jewish circles, Joseph, the favorite son of Jacob, is considered the "suffering Messiah". He was actually a type of the End Time Messiah. Consider these facts: He was rejected by his own, sold for twenty shekels of silver, suffered unjustly and refused to sin (with Potifer's wife). When Joseph's brother finally turned to him for help (during the famine) they cried out for mercy. Joseph readily forgave them, embraced them, fed them and gave them the best land of Egypt. All these events in Joseph's life foreshadow the role of Jesus with His own brothers, the Jews. When it looks like all hope is lost, Jesus will save the day!

The climax of this book is the climax of human history. These events are all well represented in the New Testament. However, I have chosen to declare the coming of Mashiach ben David, Messiah son of David, in the words of the ancient Jewish prophets. This is my small way of honoring those who have suffered so much for so long. It is, after all, their story; it is, after all, their victory. [For dramatic emphasis, this portion of the book is in paragraph form.]

Zechariah 14:1-2; Psalms 83:4; Zechariah 14:3; Isaiah 52:7; Zechariah 14:4; Zechariah 12:10; Joel 3:16-17.

THE CLIMAX OF HUMAN HISTORY

Behold, the Day of the Lord is coming. For I will gather all the nations to battle against Jerusalem. The city shall be taken, the houses rifled and the women ravished. They (the nations) have said, "Come, and let us cut them off from being a nation, that the name of Israel may be remembered no more".

Then the Lord will go forth and fight against those nations.

In that day the Lord will defend the inhabitants of Jerusalem; It shall be in that day that I (Messiah) will seek to destroy all the nations that come against Jerusalem.

How beautiful upon the mountains are the feet of Him who brings good news. And in that Day His feet will stand on the Mount of Olives, which faces Jerusalem on the east. Then they will look upon Me whom they pierced. Yes, they will mourn for Him as one mourns for His only Son, and grieve for Him as one grieves for a firstborn.

The Lord also will roar from Zion, and utter His voice from Jerusalem; the heavens and earth will shake; but the Lord will be a shelter for His people, and the strength of the children of Israel. So you shall know that I am the Lord your God, dwelling in Zion, My holy mountain.

THE DENOUEMENT

Mid-Tribulation, Satan and his minions were cast to earth.

Michael and his angels warred with Satan. It took time. It took a war. Jesus' power is so much greater than the power of the angels.

Notice how easily Jesus overpowers the Antichrist.

> [8] *And then the lawless one will be revealed,* **whom the Lord will consume with the breath of His mouth and destroy with the brightness of His coming.**
>
> 2 Thessalonians 2:8 (emphasis added)

The once powerful Antichrist, now totally disabled, is easily dispatched into the lake of fire, along with the false prophet. They will never be heard from again.

> [20] *Then the beast was captured, and with him the false prophet who worked signs in his presence, by which he deceived those who received the mark of the beast and those who worshiped his image. These two were cast alive into the lake of fire burning with brimstone.*
>
> Revelation 19:20

Although some authors use the terms "hell" (bottomless pit) and "lake of fire" interchangeably, it is evident from Revelation that hell is a holding tank, so to speak, before one receives his final judgment. We recall that "death and hell" represent a place, and also two evil spirits (page 95).

The end game for the spirits "death and hell" is the lake of fire.

> [14] *Then Death and Hades were cast into the lake of fire. This is the second death.*
>
> Revelation 20:14

Likewise, the end game for unsaved people is the lake of fire. [These people's soul's are currently in hell, waiting to be reunited with their bodies Revelation 20:13].

> [15] *And anyone not found written in the Book of Life was cast into the lake of fire.*
>
> Revelation 20:15

Satan will not be reunited with the evil duo for a thousand years. He goes to the bottomless pit (hell) to wait until the Millennium is concluded.

> [2] *He laid hold of the dragon, that serpent of old, who is the Devil and Satan, and bound him for a thousand years;*
> [3] *and he cast him into the bottomless pit, and shut him up, and set a seal on him, so that he should deceive the nations no more till the thousand years were finished.* ***But after these things he must be released for a little while.***
> Revelation 20:2-3 (emphasis added)

There is so much more to tell. The Millennial Reign is only the beginning. The lion will lay down with the lamb and men will learn war no more. But what else?

Another war of Gog and Magog is referenced in Revelation 20:8 after the Millennial Reign. Then the earth must be purified by fire. The Father and New Jerusalem will come down and dwell forever on the new earth.

> [1] *Now I saw a new heaven and a new earth, for the first heaven and the first earth had passed away. Also there was no more sea.* [2]*Then I, John, saw the holy city, New Jerusalem, coming down out of heaven from God, prepared as a bride adorned for her husband.* [3]*And I heard a loud voice from heaven saying, "Behold, the tabernacle of God is with men, and He will dwell with them, and they shall be His people, God Himself will be with them and be their God.*
> Revelation 21:1-3

Before the Father comes down and eternity begins, sinners must face God at the Great White Throne Judgment.

They must then be cast into the lake of fire which is the "second death". I believe those living on the earth during eternity will be able to see into the lake of fire. Notice the Book of Isaiah closes with this grim picture of suffering sinners.

> [22] *"For as the new heavens and the new earth*
> *Which I will make shall remain before Me", says*
> *the Lord,"So shall your descendants and your*
> *name remain.*
> [23] *And it shall come to pass*
> *That from one New Moon to another,*
> *And from one Sabbath to another,*
> *All flesh shall come to worship before Me", says*
> *the Lord*
> [24] **"And they shall go forth and look**
> **Upon the corpses of the men**
> **Who have transgressed against Me.**
> **For their worm does not die,**
> **And their fire is not quenched.**
> **They shall be an abhorrence to all flesh".**
> Isaiah 66:22-24 (emphasis added)

That is why the primary purpose of every committed Christian, throughout the world, throughout the ages, should always be the same: to take the good news of Jesus Christ to the nations. The good news is this: You do not have to go to the White Throne Judgment—you can confess Jesus to escape the judgment called the lake of fire.

Here's The Good News

The Church will be taken into heaven before the Tribulation and Jesus wants you to be one of those who escapes the wrath to come. Being a member of the Church of Jesus Christ is not a matter of what denomination you belong to, or where you go to church. To be a member of His Church, or His Body, is determined by the intent of your heart, which only God can see. If you are unsure of your status with God, say this prayer with genuine conviction.

Heavenly Father, I know I am a sinner. Though I've fallen short of Your glory so many times, I truly believe that Jesus died on the cross so that I (state your name) could have eternal salvation. Jesus, I thank you for dying on the cross for me. I invite you now to come into my heart, take over my life and show me Your will for my life. I promise that from this day forward, I will live for You and follow Your plan for my life. Fill me with Your Holy Spirit and empower me to do Your will. Amen.

Epilogue

What is God's eternal purpose for the Church? The Church is the mystery that has been hidden from ages and generations, as it says so beautifully in Colossians chapter one.

> *²⁶ the mystery which has been hidden from ages and from generations, but now has been revealed to His saints. ²⁷ To them God willed to make known what are the riches of the glory of this mystery among the Gentiles: which is Christ in you, the hope of glory.*
>
> Colossians 1:26, 27

Adam and Eve had been created *"crowned with glory and honor"* (Psalm 8:5). Unfortunately, they fell into sin, and this glory departed and they were naked.

> *²³ for all have sinned and fall short of the glory of God,*
>
> Romans 3:23

Fortunately, God exercised a plan formulated before the foundation of the world. God sent the Man, Jesus Christ His only Son, to die for us, while we were yet sinners. When God raised Jesus from the dead, He seated Him at His right hand...

> *²⁰ which He worked in Christ when He raised Him from the dead and seated Him at His right hand in the heavenly places, ²¹ far above all principality and power and might and dominion, and every name that is named, not only in this age but also in that which is to come.*
>
> Ephesians 1:20, 21

Where are those principalities, powers, mights and dominions today? They rule over the earth out of the Satanic kingdom in the second heaven. Satan's right to rule came from Adam, who committed high treason when he ate the forbidden fruit. However, the demonic powers will be cast down to earth midway through the Tribulation, when man's 6,000 year dominion of planet earth expires. Three and a half years after that, they will be cast into hell with Satan (Revelation 20:1-3).

Who will replace principalities, powers, mights and dominions, as rulers over natural men? God the Father alone has the right to delegate this authority, and He gave it to Jesus.

> *¹⁸ And Jesus came and spoke to them, saying, "All*

authority has been given to Me in heaven and on earth".

Matthew 28:18

The fact that Jesus is seated at the right hand of the Father indicates He has all authority in the Universe. That is the significance of the term, "The Right Hand".

[1] *A Psalm of David. The Lord said to my Lord, "Sit at My right hand, Till I make Your enemies Your footstool".*

Psalm 110:1

However, Jesus willingly shares this power with the Body of Christ.

[22] *And He put all things under His feet, and gave Him to be head over all things to the church,* [23] **which is His body, the fullness of Him who fills all in all.**

Ephesians1:22, 23 (emphasis added)

John MacMillan, in <u>The Authority of the Believer</u>, explains who will replace the demonic powers in the second heaven. "When they [the Church] have approved themselves, they will in actuality take the seats of the 'powers of the air,' thereby superseding those who have manifested their unfitness and unworthiness. This purpose, present and future, is very definitely stated in Ephesians 3:9-11". [22]

[9] *and to make all see what is the fellowship of the mystery, which from the beginning of the ages has been hidden in God who created all things through Jesus Christ;* [10] *to the intent that now the manifold wisdom of God might be made known by the church to the principalities and powers in the heavenly places,* [11] *according to the eternal purpose which He accomplished in Christ Jesus our Lord,*

That being the case, we can understand why we wrestle against principalities, powers and rulers of darkness. MacMillan explains further. "It is consequently not strange that the principalities and powers who are to be dispossessed of the seats of authority now occupied by themselves should savagely resist their own displacement". [23]

Let us consider our exalted destiny, as described in the Book of Revelation:

1. Kings and priests

> [6] *and has made us kings and priests to His God and Father, to Him be glory and dominion forever and ever. Amen.*
>
> Revelation 1:6

2. Reign "over" the earth

> [5] *"And hast formed them into a Kingdom to be priests to our God, And they reign over the earth".*
>
> Revelation 5:10 (WNT)

3. Rule the nations

> [26] *And he who overcomes, and keeps My works until the end, to him I will give power over the nations*
>
> Revelation 2:26

This ministry of the Church will be eternal. As the human family in natural bodies lives on in perpetuity, we continue to rule in glory forever.

> [20] *Now to Him who is able to do exceedingly abundantly above all that we ask or think, according to the power that works in us, to Him be glory in the church by Christ Jesus to all generations, forever and ever. Amen.*
>
> Ephesians 3:20, 21

We are now proceeding into a time of maximum danger, as we conclude the "end times". There will be persecution. We need to keep our eye on the prize. In distant ages yet to come, we will travel the universe with Jesus. We will walk in the glory realm with Him. No future generation will enjoy the privileges we have, as the "Bride of Christ".

Let's add a few words to John Newton's classic song of praise, "Amazing Grace", to make the picture clear.

"When we've been there

ten thousand (10 million, 10 billion, 10 trillion) years

Bright shining as the sun.

We've no less days to sing God's praise,

Than when we'd first begun".

(World without end, Amen.)

Endnotes

[1] Jeffrey Satinover, M.D., Cracking the Bible Code, Harper Collins Publishers, Inc., New York, New York, pages 273 and 275, 1998

[2] Kenneth Copeland, Living at the End of Time— A Time of Supernatural Increase. Kenneth Copeland Publications, pages 20, 21, 22, 1997, 1998

[3] Dr. Billye Brim, "The Glory Watch", page 13, Spring 2002, A Glorious Church Fellowship, Branson, Missouri

[4] David Baron, Zechariah, A Commentary on His Visions and Prophecies, reprint, Kregel Publications, Grand Rapids, Michigan 1956, page 327

[5] Ibid, page 327

[6] Belleville News Democrat, "Divisions in Islam rooted in actions of followers after death of Mohammed", Sunday, March 23, 2003, page 7A, Belleville, Illinois

[7] "Union for the Mediterranean," Ask.com, modified 10 December 2013, Wikipedia

[8] Op cit, Baron, page 176

[9] Ibid pages 179

[10] Belleville News Democrat, "Purported Al Qaida message warns of attacks", page 5A, June 8, 2004, Belleville, Illinois

[11] Op cit, Baron, page 182

[12] David Baron, Israel in the Plan of God, Kregel Publications, Grand Rapids, Micigan 1983, page 283

[13] E. W. Bullinger, The Companion Bible, Kregel Publications, Grand Rapids, Michigan, 1922, page 846

[14] Clarence Larkin, Dispensational Truth Or God's Plan and Purpose for the Ages, 1918, page 145

[15] David Baron, Types, Psalms and Prophecies, reprint, Keren Ahvah Meshihit, 91103 Jerusalem, Israel, page 23

[16] Mike Bickle, "The Book of Revelation", Free Teaching Library, www.mikebickle.org

[17] Sister Jeanne Wilkerson as quoted on Dr. Billye Brimm teaching tape series

[18] Adiv Sternman, "PM lashes out at 'anti-Semitic' Israel Critics, Times of Israel, May 28, 2013

Endnotes Continued

[19] Reza Khalili, "Ayatolla: Kill all Jews, annihilate Israel", World Net Daily, 2/5/12

[20] Mike Bickle, "The Book of Revelation", Free Teaching Library, www.mikebickle.org

[21] R. Edwin Herman, Bible Code Bombshell, New Leaf Press, Green Forest, AR 72638, page 133

[22] Shahar Ilan, "Does a clone have a soul?"/Haaretz.com, Saturday, August 6, 2005, page 1

[23] John MacMillan, The Authority of the Believer, Hope,Faith,Prayer. com